Illuminating the
Secret Revelation of John

Westar Studies

The Westar Studies series offers distinctive scholarly publications on topics related to the field of Religious Studies. The studies seek to be multi-dimensional both in terms of the subject matter addressed and the perspective of the author. Westar Studies are not related to Westar seminars but offer scholars a deliberate space of free inquiry to engage both scholarly peers and the public.

Illuminating the
Secret Revelation of John

Catching the Light

Shirley Paulson

CASCADE *Books* · Eugene, Oregon

ILLUMINATING THE SECRET REVELATION OF JOHN
Catching the Light

Westar Studies

Cascade Books
An Imprint of Wipf and Stock Publishers
199 W. 8th Ave., Suite 3
Eugene, OR 97401

www.wipfandstock.com

PAPERBACK ISBN: 978-1-6667-3012-8
HARDCOVER ISBN: : 978-1-6667-2122-5
EBOOK ISBN: 978-1-6667-2123-2

Cataloguing-in-Publication data:

Names: Paulson, Shirley, author.

Title: Illuminating the Secret Revelation of John / Shirley Paulson.

Description: Eugene, OR: Cascade Books, 2022. | Westar Studies. | Includes bibliographical references and index.

Identifiers: ISBN 978-1-6667-3012-8 (paperback). | ISBN 978-1-6667-2122-5 (hardcover). | ISBN 978-1-6667-2123-2 (ebook).

Subjects: LSCH: Apocryphon of John—Criticism, interpretation, etc.| Gnostic literature—Relation to the Old Testament. | Apocryphal books—New Testament—Criticism, interpretation, etc.

Classification: BT1392.A752 P38 2022 (print). | BT1392.A752 (ebook).

Permissions and Credit Lines

TEXTS

The Holy Bible containing the Old and New Testaments: New Revised Standard Version, New York: Oxford University Press, 1989. Used by permission.

King, Karen L. *The Secret Revelation of John*. Cambridge: Harvard University Press, 2006. Used by permission.

Layton, Bentley. *The Gnostic Scriptures: Ancient Wisdom for the New Age*. The Anchor Bible Reference Library. New York: Doubleday, 1987. Used by permission.

Meyer, Marvin, ed. *The Nag Hammadi Scriptures: The Revised and Updated Translation of Sacred Gnostic Texts*. International ed. New York: HarperCollins, 2007. Used by permission.

IMAGES

Maps of the Roman Empire (Figure 1), Alexandria (Figure 5), and Nag Hammadi (Figure 7) provided by Manna Bible Maps. Used by permission.

Figure 2: Interior of the Great Library of Alexandria. Nineteenth-century artistic rendering by O. van Corven, based on some archaeological evidence (Wikimedia Commons [https://commons.wikimedia.org/wiki/Category:Library_of_Alexandria/]; image in the public domain).

Figure 3: *Gemma Augustea*: Roman cameo, onyx, 9–12 CE. Gold frame, seventeenth century. Vienna. Photo courtesy of the Kunsthistorisches Museum, Vienna.

Figure 4: Hierarchical Society of the Roman Empire (image designed by the author).

Figure 5: The Jewish quarter in Alexandria, Egypt (courtesy of Manna Bible Maps).

Figure 6: The Nag Hammadi Codices. This image is housed digitally in the Institute for Antiquity and Christianity at Claremont College (Honnold/Mudd) in Claremont, California.

Figure 8: Folio 32 of Nag Hammadi Codex II, with the ending of the Apocryphon of John, and the beginning of the Gospel of Thomas (Wikimedia Commons [https://commons.wikimedia.org/wiki/File:Nag_Hammadi_Codex_II.jpg/]; image in the public domain).

Figure 9: Simplified Structure of the Heavenly Realm (image designed by the author).

Figure 10: Yaldabaoth, the Chief Ruler (Wikipedia [https://en.wikipedia.org/wiki/Demiurge]; image in the public domain)

Dedicated
to my husband, Richard, for his unwavering support
and
to Lois Rae Carlson, CSB, for her conviction in the continuity of good

Contents

Figures

Preface

I remember vividly the day the Secret Revelation of John nudged its way into my life. It happened in early 2003, while I was sitting in the office of my seminary advisor, George Kalantzis. He was an excellent listener, and after giving me the space to explain my thoughts about God, Christ, and the power of spiritual healing, he stepped away and pulled his copy of the Secret Revelation of John off the shelf. He asked if I'd ever read it. No, I had never heard of it.

"Good," he said, "read it before you read anybody else's commentary on it. Then, decide for yourself what it means." I read it several times, each time feeling like I was drawing closer to a remarkable treasure just beyond my grasp. But like almost everyone else who picks it up, I kept running into an impenetrable forest of strange words and ideas.

A powerful message of healing and hope shone through, and finally I knew it was time to listen to the voices of scholars who had studied it before me. Karen King announced in her 2006 monograph, *The Secret Revelation of John*, that "the importance of the *Secret Revelation of John* can hardly be overestimated."[1] Fifteen years later, after reading the views of many scholars, and pursuing my own ideas about it, I'm more convinced than ever of its extraordinary value.

I wrote my doctoral thesis as a critical conversation on the healing theologies in Christian Science (my faith tradition) and the Secret Revelation of John.[2] My supervisors, Karen Wenell and Stephen Pattison, challenged me to wrestle with both the text itself and my personal reaction to it. Themes of healing surfaced easily for me. But its jarring transport through time and space, the transformation of characters and their identities, the

---

1. King, *The Secret Revelation of John*, vii.
2. Paulson, "Healing Theologies in Christian Science and Secret Revelation of John."

power of demons, and allusions to an ancient culture often threw me off course.

My family and nonscholarly (but very smart) friends became an important part of the publication of this book, because in my earliest attempts to show them the sparkling treasures within the Secret Revelation of John, their eyes would go dull, and I'd lose them! They, too, couldn't get past the impenetrable forest. But I knew they would love it, if only I could find a way to light a path for them. My husband, Richard, was my best critic and conversation partner during all the years it took for this book to take shape.

Hilary Barner is one of those friends who read my manuscript without any prior knowledge of the Secret Revelation of John and told me where the language slipped into confounding scholarese. I hope she and my friends have succeeded in helping this book find its way into the hands and hearts of people who will treasure it.

I also had the good fortune of enlisting the support, scholarly wisdom, and experience of scholars Hal Taussig, Deborah Niederer Saxon, Stephanie Duzant, and Celene Lillie, who already valued the Secret Revelation of John. They see this project as a foundational study for biblical, theological, and religious scholars and professors, and they have held me to the scholarly standards they and their colleagues should expect. I can't say enough about the contributions and insightful support I received from my Westar editor, Arthur Dewey. He read and critiqued each version of the manuscript, but more importantly, he was an inspired and crucial conversation partner who encouraged me to tackle some of the tougher topics I hadn't even considered.

In order to meet the needs of both the general public and curious scholars, some compromises were made that need explanation here. Scholars know that all of the codices from the Nag Hammadi collection were damaged when they were discovered, leaving significant lacunae in some parts of the texts. Usually, the missing letters and words are noted in brackets where translators have surmised the meaning. Due to this book's goal of focusing on the meaning of the text, all the distracting brackets and textual difficulties have been removed. However, since all translated portions are referenced by page or chapter and verse, scholars may confirm these details from the original translations listed in the Sources Cited.

I also took the liberty to use multiple translations, selecting whichever one could provide the clearest meaning. Permission was granted for extensive use of translations in King's, Layton's, and Meyer's books.

Another clarification should be noted concerning the existence of a shorter and longer version of the Secret Revelation of John itself (more commonly known as the Apocryphon of John in academic circles). I presented the story line as if it were one, but in fact two of the extant versions are longer and include material that is not included in the two extant shorter versions. Although I generally use the longer version, I occasionally mix them—again, for the purpose of avoiding confusion for the first-time reader. Karen King has provided an excellent parallel reading of the longer and shorter versions in her book for a comparison between the two versions.

Finally, an important tool I have provided to help modern readers find meaning is my full paraphrase of the longer version, located at the back of the book. As with any paraphrase, it should not be read as a translation, because the paraphrase skips over details that are nearly meaningless in contemporary culture. If this paraphrase can help readers find their way into the heart of the text, a full translation from other sources will help them study the details more accurately.

My hope is that I have smoothed over the rough path between twenty-first-century and second-century readers, so that the light, wisdom, and healing power from the Secret Revelation of John may fulfill its purpose—at least in part—again in this age.

I

Alexandria!
Not Rome, Not Jerusalem

A strange and ancient book has been moving from the bookshelves of scholars and into the hands of curious and (often) Christian thinkers and spiritual seekers. Even though scholars have been able to read the Secret Revelation of John[1] since it came to light in 1945,[2] the odd images of the Yaldabaoth god, the Mother Barbelō, and the unwise Wisdom have left most modern readers scratching their heads.[3] The title is rather obscure, its logic appears to run in circles, and many people say it's one of those "gnostic" heresies. Understandably, many churchgoers have found little incentive to pick it up. But since scholars have been chipping away at these outer obstacles and polishing the rough gems, they've come to realize this book is of great value, *especially* to those who love the Bible!

1. Scholars also refer to the book as the Apocryphon of John or sometimes as the Secret Book of John.

2. The Secret Revelation of John is one of the fifty-two texts that were discovered in a cave near Nag Hammadi, Egypt, in 1945. That collection of codices (ancient books) is commonly referred to as the Nag Hammadi Library.

3. Reading the Secret Revelation of John even in English translation is not a simple task. Some readers may find it easier to approach the text by first reading this book as it is laid out, with its cultural setting and explanations for contemporary perspectives. Others may prefer to begin with the paraphrase of the text near the end of this book, to get a feel for what the Secret Revelation of John is all about.

The purpose of this book is to pick up the polished gems and look at them carefully in the light of our modern experiences and historical perspectives. To do so, we'll drop in for a visit in the city where all the forces came together to give it birth in the second century. Religion teachers, philosophers, Christ-followers,[4] Jews, and students flocked to this cultural center of the world. No, not Rome, and not Jerusalem. But they converged on Alexandria, the great city situated along the north coast of Egypt and founded by Alexander the Great centuries before Jesus was born. All the constituent parts of the Secret Revelation of John cohabitate in second-century Alexandria, as we'll see after we listen to a few of the people we encounter.

FIGURE 1

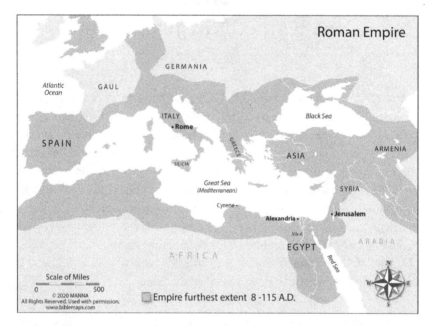

Alexandria, Jerusalem, and Rome
(courtesy of Manna Bible Maps)

4. People who followed Christ Jesus in the second century were seldom called Christians. That name came later. The closest terms for identifying this group of people would be either "Jesus-followers" or "Christ-followers." "Jesus-followers" conveys the importance of the man they followed, whereas "Christ-followers" may represent the adoption of his teachings.

After getting acquainted with second-century Alexandrian life, we'll look at the way the Secret Revelation of John speaks to the heart of twenty-first-century readers as well. Then we'll start to explore the text itself. The bulk of the book is organized like a kind of literary museum, where we can pause to think about some of the most important contributions to our lives today. We won't be able to see all the possibilities, but there will be enough to whet our appetite for returning again and again.

WELCOME TO SECOND-CENTURY ALEXANDRIA

We want to start our tour in second-century Alexandria, because the Secret Revelation of John was written for people who were looking for answers to life's tough questions of the time, a period of formidable upheaval. In the midst of political and social turbulence, people tend to seek a deeper understanding of their own identity, their communities, the divine Being, and the universe. This is the state of Alexandria we are about to encounter.

Alexandrians understood well the confluence of Roman, Greek, Egyptian, and Jewish customs. This city, known for its attraction to writers and thinkers, seems to have been the perfect spawning ground for the radically new, but Christ-based, ideas in the Secret Revelation of John.

If we could walk through the neatly laid out streets of this bustling port city in the second century, we might be startled to discover such a visible blending of the multicultured way of life. The great Library, the cultural center of the city, explains much of the draw for teachers and students throughout the Mediterranean area who are eager to learn philosophy, rhetoric, religion, science, or some other scholarly subject. The Library, a part of the vast Alexandrian Museum complex, holds the largest collection of papyrus scrolls in the world and functions like a modern interactive research center with a zoo, an observatory, and a medical laboratory. Greek philosophers belonging to all sorts of schools from Stoicism to Epicureanism have flocked to Alexandria and mingle readily with the Egyptian cosmologists and those who practice mystery religions. A large community of Jews have settled here too, since the destruction of their temple in 70 CE forced even more of them to flee Jerusalem, augmenting the numbers already in Alexandria.

FIGURE 2

Interior of the Great Library of Alexandria. Nineteenth-century artistic rendering by
O. van Corven, based on some archaeological evidence
(Wikimedia Commons; image in the public domain).

But the very success of this great metropolis may have also become the
source of its heartache. Rome, over a thousand miles away, has installed its
military authority throughout the Mediterranean area, but it is especially
tough with Alexandria. Compared with Alexandria's fertile ground for
research, questioning, thinking, and writing, Rome and its preoccupation
with conquest and gladiator entertainment presents a stark contrast. Here
is an image of Roman attitudes toward success:

FIGURE 3

Gemma Augustea: Roman cameo, onyx, 9–12 CE. Gold frame, seventeenth century. Vienna. Photo courtesy of the Kunsthistorisches Museum, Vienna.

This Roman cameo, known as the *Gemma Augustea,* was carved in approximately 10–20 CE. It poignantly captures the contrast between the superior and dominant Romans (in the top half) and the people they have subdued throughout the Roman Empire (in the bottom half). In the image, the beam lifted in the lower left was the type used in victory parades with one of the prominent captives bound to it for display in the parade.

However, all the measures of Alexandrian success continue to threaten the Roman imperialists, who retaliate with ever-tighter domination over this second-largest city in the world. We can't miss the heavy imprint of Rome's conquest in everyday life. Ever since the Romans gained control of Egypt, some thirty years before Jesus's birth, Alexandria's huge production of grain and its largest port in the world had together made it the breadbasket for Rome. A century later, when the Flavian dynasty (69–96) controlled Egypt, the emperor had become so dependent on the produce from its wealthiest city, Alexandria, that he took it for granted as his personal territory.

From beyond Rome in the West to Asia in the East, this Mediterranean jewel attracted attention. A thriving Jewish community had already settled in Alexandria long before, along with Greeks and other foreigners. No wonder multitudes of Jews found their way to this prospering city hundreds of miles away when Emperor Titus destroyed their temple in Jerusalem and the city along with it in the year 70! The new migrant Jews joined those already established, tried to rebuild their lives, and contributed to the Alexandrian prestige. It had become the world center of Jewish religion and culture.

But the next Jewish-Alexandrian generation could no longer tolerate intensifying Roman oppression. When exploitation reached the breaking point, rebellion became the next alternative. Failing to find any relief, thousands of Jews rose up in desperate rebellion once again. But they ultimately perished at the overpowering hands of the Roman military during the so-called Rebellion of the Exile of 115–117.

By now, the Jewish communities in Egypt are effectively diminished. And yet we understand why they're still fighting. It's a fight for survival against the incessant oppression of and aggressive control over Jews. Above all, though, they're fighting for their God, the God who brought them out of bondage a couple of millennia before.

Many of the Jews who had become faithful followers of Jesus probably perished along with their fellow rebelling Jews,[5] but the painful losses for everyone rearranged precarious relationships among the people of Alexandria as they searched in all directions for solace and guidance. A mounting anti-Jewish attitude has been pressuring the Jewish Jesus-followers to separate themselves from their traditional Jewish colleagues, causing them to sort out their own relationships with their Greek and Roman neighbors.

These Jews are eager to engage in conversation with the ubiquitous Greek philosophers and teachers of religion, as all of them respond to the human outcry. As they look more deeply into their own teachings and traditions, their search is not a scholastic, intellectual exercise. It is a response to the hard questions of the day: How can we survive war? What is the meaning of soul? Who is God, and what happens after death? How is God both good and omnipotent? Is healing related to salvation? How does anyone cope with Roman oppression?

---

5. For a fuller description of these relationships, see Boyarin, *Dying for God*. He argues that "various strands of Judaism and Christianity overlapped with each other rather than being separate monolithic entities" (Boyarin, *Dying for God*, 8, 21).

Pausing to listen to some of the teachers around the city, it is no surprise that we run across the full gamut of answers to these urgent questions—answers from Stoics, Jews, astrologists, demonologists, and various groups studying Plato's philosophical writings, which were enjoying an upswing in popularity. Christ-followers too are offering answers to the big questions. Among these was the teacher who had just finished writing his seminal work, the Secret Revelation of John.

Now we stop to listen intently. It could be his broad knowledge of Greek, Roman, Egyptian, and Jewish culture that attracts both Jews and non-Jews to his school, but his message is clearly a Christ-centered, Jewish one. The saving power inherent in his Christ message originates in Jewish teachings, but he uses non-Jewish customs and philosophies to demonstrate the power of Christ.

Naturally, the soldiers, sent from Rome to keep control in Alexandria are nervous when they pick up on any implications of a disrupted hierarchical order. Claiming superiority for *any* power outside the Roman patriarchal order threatens Roman hegemony.[6] But we can discern a subversive and hidden message from this teacher. It makes sense to people who have lived among the conquered populations, and yet the Roman supervisors may or may not fully grasp what these pupils and this teacher are talking about.[7]

6. This panoramic overview of second-century Alexandria gives a broad image of everyday life in this corner of the world, but some of the areas of city life are worthy of a more penetrating look. Elliott's *Family Empires* takes readers into the heart of Roman-era households to feel the dynamic role of Roman influence on a more visceral level.

7. Scott's *Domination and the Arts of Resistance* is a valuable resource explaining the shifts in conversation and behavior among the enslaved communities in relation to their dominant rulers. Knowledge of what Scott terms "hidden transcripts" helps modern readers understand some of the meaning of *secret* messages or the double meaning of certain terms used in ancient texts such as the Secret Revelation of John.

FIGURE 4

Hierarchical Society
of the Roman Empire

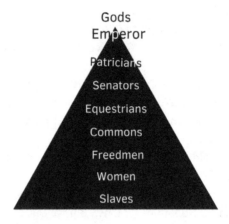

The Roman Empire, starting with the emperor himself and including the whole cosmos, operates as a strictly hierarchical order. Although the divine remains supreme over all, human power originates from the emperor and descends to the Patricians (those with the highest advisory positions and great wealth), next to the Senators (with political power from ancestral lineage and wealth), and down to the Equestrians (possessing secure minimum worth and involved in various types of businesses), descending further to the Commons (all other freeborn Roman citizens with the right to legal marriage with other Roman citizens), and finally to the Freedpeople (men and women who earned or won their way out of slavery). Women subserve men, and children are governed by nonenslaved adults. Below all of them, at the lowest rank, are the enslaved (usually those whose families had been captured in Roman conquests). They are the most numerous members of society, but they have no authority even over their own lives.

In the setting of this gathering of students around a teacher, however, a quick glance at the clothing of the learners clues us into the fact that they come from all social classes. We see how easily fellowship flows among the classes, including between the enslaved and those from higher stations. There is good reason for the Romans to be nervous about these students and their teacher. Not only his message of equal worth, but also

8

the common Greek language and culture, serves to unify master and pupils, classes and ethnic groups. Even the Jews who fled to Alexandria from Judea are more fluent in Greek than Aramaic now, so it is not surprising that the sacred texts were translated from Hebrew into Greek here in Alexandria.

This school, like most of the other small groups of pupils with their teachers, primarily uses the Greek version of the Hebrew Bible, known as the *Septuagint*. Although some of the pupils are Jewish, most of the newer students come from a Greco-Roman background, knowing only the Greek and Roman gods. The sacred Jewish text, in combination with the powerful and transforming ideas they hear from this teacher concerning the teachings of Jesus of Nazareth, draw them in fellowship with these Christ-following Jews. Some Gentile philosophers in Alexandria have also begun to introduce the Jewish God into their own teachings, inspiring many Greeks throughout the city to find their way to the Christ-following teachers.

Despite the teachers' deep interest in the teachings from the *Septuagint*, the resurgent interest in Plato has also grabbed the attention of the wider population. Greeks themselves recognize how the ideas from his *Timaeus* and *Parminides* take on new relevance five hundred years later in the heat of ever-increasing Roman oppression. Our teacher recognizes the influence of these Hellenized intellectuals in the struggle to reenvision social and political systems, but he uses their familiar teachings to distinguish them from his own Christ teachings.

Numerous other philosophical systems have gained popularity also. Almost everyone is conversant with Greek Stoicism, because it offers practical solutions, especially to the problem of ubiquitous demons. You can't really see demons, but you know their existence by the feelings they instill in you. They are like the spirit of fear that takes over during a terrible storm, or great anger when someone with higher power abuses you.

People know these demons well—hundreds of them—because they stir up passions at just about any time or place, causing diseases and every form of human suffering. Since no one, from enslaved people to patricians, can escape the torment of demons, the Stoic solution of learning to control one's own passions resonates with people of all classes.

However, one of the most important *secrets* of the Secret Revelation of John may well be that its author sees a direct link between the action of these unseen powers (demons) and the work of the Roman emperor's minions. Gaining control of the demons might provide the key that unlocks the secrets of the power behind Rome, as well as the painful personal effects of demons.

The author of the Secret Revelation of John takes advantage of another source of support for the mastery of the demons. Local Egyptian scholars lecture particularly well on the all-important relationship between human body parts and numerous divinities and demons. Their popular *Hermetic Vulgata* offers a vast knowledge of the names of demons, and since demons can be exorcised through addressing them by name, this enormously helpful resource supports exorcists of all types.

Another Egyptian scholar, Ptolemy (100–170), continues to convert the worldviews of religious leaders, philosophers, and teachers through his well-known work in mathematics and astronomy. As he refocuses attention to the heavenly motion, he realigns their view of the universe. And now we notice how a combination of his (Ptolemy's) new astronomy with Aristotle's physics from five hundred years earlier is widely accepted. It is both practical truth and religious doctrine.

Crosscurrents of science, philosophy, and religion evoke creative ideas about God and the world, humanity and health, and the meaning of life. Our teacher encourages discussion on topics as broad as cosmology, anthropology, health, and ethics, because all of them relate to the larger picture of salvation. As most of the teachers of Alexandria do, this teacher also makes a wide variety of materials available to his pupils, including diverse philosophical and sacred traditions, astrology, magic, asceticism, baptismal experiences, and studies on exorcism and healing. As he nimbly weaves his way through the treacherous shoals of Roman threats, demonic powers, and religious contradictions, we hear a remarkable blend of imagery from Greek philosophy, Jewish scriptures, and Egyptian influences.

But his lectures always lead back to the teachings of Jesus. Whether he's criticizing Jewish and Greek customs or drawing on their stories and myths, he persistently demonstrates how Christ provides the ultimate answers to their questions. He talks about a salvation from suffering and darkness. It's also a salvation that inspires all people to live together in harmony. The more we listen to this teacher, the more amazed we become. Unlike any other teacher, this man has woven together the greatest mysteries of the world. Who else has described the action of God's creation and all of cosmology, its relationship to the world we live in, and the way Christ alone is able to finally save from all evil in completeness and perfection? No one!

Ever! These are truly the gems of Christ we had never noticed before, never realized their great beauty and worth.

Walking home after the class through the vast Jewish quarters, we can't help but wonder about these Jews. They make up almost a fifth of the city population, and although some have contributed more broadly to the great cosmopolitan mix, others remain in closed communities, adhering to very strict ethnic behaviors. Our teacher leans heavily on their sacred texts, especially Genesis. But most of them think it's too jarring to rethink what Moses said about creation. They don't want to hear of it.

FIGURE 5

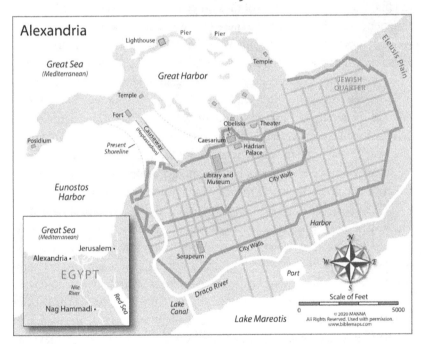

The Jewish quarter in Alexandria, Egypt
(courtesy of Manna Bible Maps).

Their isolation may contribute to their vulnerability in times of crisis. On the one hand, they and the Christ-following Jews were all persecuted together during the horror of the Roman-led Rebellion of the Exile (115–117). But on the other hand, that agonizing event began to drive a wedge between the two groups.

One of those Christ-following Jewish teachers, Justin (100–165), exemplifies this sad separation between the Jewish sects. We can't tell for sure whether Justin has ever stopped to converse with our teacher, the author of the Secret Revelation of John. But Justin makes his position quite clear in his own book, *Dialogue with Trypho, a Jew,* that the purpose of Jewish scripture is to prophesy Jesus, and the Jews who don't see that are simply wrong.

On the other hand, our teacher has another way of regarding his ancient heritage in the Secret Revelation of John. Some of the earlier Hebrew texts inspire truth and should be taken seriously, he teaches. And some of them need second-century updating. His knowledge of the Jewish Bible and his concern for the value of these ancient, sacred texts demonstrate his proficiency and his faith. References to the Jewish book of Genesis and to Wisdom literature keep surfacing while he's talking, and it is evident that he is also drawn to the newer gospels that have been circulating about Jesus.

Conversations between the Secret Revelation author and his disciples, and between Justin and his disciples, might have also perked up our ears if either of them had ever moved to the subject of the Roman magistrates. Although it would most certainly have taken place in hushed tones, we can be sure neither one of them would have believed in the ultimate power behind the Roman atrocities. Christ-followers united behind the conviction that evil power is not of the one God but of false powers or demons.

Our teacher is drawing a lot of attention. Some of us are simply curious, but we notice students from faraway places have started listening in too. The teacher does not evade the deepest questions, such as why and how evil came to be, what God means in the midst of death and fear, and how to be saved from this evil—whether evil is identified as demons or Roman oppressors. Jews explain the cosmos and the origin of evil from their book of Genesis. But those answers are not thorough or deep enough for the Greek converts, who seek answers to new philosophical questions challenging the second century. Jesus had introduced a novel approach to his Judaean faith, and his ideas, particularly concerning the nature of the divine presence, are especially pertinent to the second-century struggles with Rome. The world has changed since Jesus's time, but his teachings of the present realm of God and dominion over evil seem to translate clearly to the current situation.

WELCOME TO THE TWENTY-FIRST-CENTURY WORLD

Almost the same could be said about the twenty-first century as the second century. That is, the world has changed since Jesus's time, but his teachings of the realm of God and dominion over evil seem to translate clearly to the current situation. Who wants to read an ancient book with multiple gods, attacking demons, two kinds of Adam, and set in such a foreign culture?

We might consider reading an ancient book if it offers new ideas that help us navigate our identity in the world of artificial intelligence, guides us through a potentially cataclysmic climate change, offers equitable health-care, and even reduces time-related stress.

Modern-day ideas such as these are some of the enduring gems from the Secret Revelation of John that we'll stop to investigate. For unknown reasons, the Secret Revelation of John and other texts important to Christ-followers disappeared within a couple of hundred years of being written down, not to be seen for another sixteen hundred years or more. Copies of the Secret Revelation of John had already circulated at least as far as from Egypt to France, and probably farther.[8] What happened to these texts and all the others discovered in Nag Hammadi is a contentious issue. Some say they were banned; others say readers simply lost interest. But now they look like treasures to both scholars and current followers of Jesus.

We can imagine the thrill of the archaeologists and scholars who first saw the ancient papyri in 1945 and realized what they were looking at!

8. For a more thorough record of when and where the ancient text, the Secret Revelation of John, might have been read, see King, *The Secret Revelation of John*, 5, 9–12.

FIGURE 6

This is the collection of ancient codices known as the Nag Hammadi Library. The Secret Revelation of John appears in three of them. This photo is housed digitally in the Institute for Antiquity and Christianity at Claremont College, Claremont, California (https://ccdl.claremont.edu/digital/collection/nha/id/1617/rec/1).

But, as with most major discoveries from ancient times, a huge amount of work lies between the discovery and the understanding of what it means.

These ancient texts had been hidden and buried in the sands of eastern Egypt, near Nag Hammadi, which is about five hundred miles south of Alexandria.

But what did they mean? In our age of instant cell-phone translators, it is hard to realize the difficulty involved in removing the roughened outer layers of these gems. Brittle and broken pages of papyri,[9] the ancient Coptic language, and centuries of cultural sea changes all contributed to challenges for the translators. Although all of the texts in the Nag Hammadi collection (sometimes called the Nag Hammadi library) were written in Coptic, there is a good possibility many or all of them were copies of original texts composed in Greek. And when they first came to light, few scholars were familiar with Coptic.

9. Papyrus was the writing surface used in the construction of books. Papyri (the plural form of *papyrus*) also refers to the sheets of papyrus joined together side by side to form codices (books). This form of publishing marked a major difference from the ancient Hebrew tradition of creating scrolls.

FIGURE 7

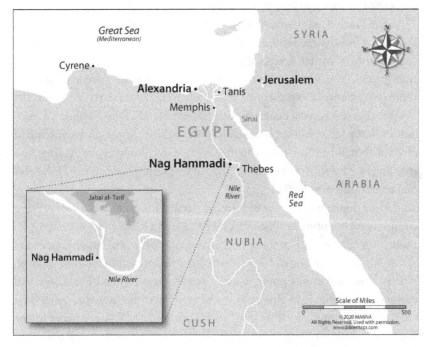

**Nag Hammadi, Egypt, the site of the discovery of the collection of codices
(courtesy of Manna Bible Maps)**

Furthermore, dealing with the Coptic version of a lost Greek text is not the only difficulty for translators. Even if the language were better known and many of the pages and words hadn't been destroyed, good translations are more than word-for-word exchanges. In order to understand the conversations in the Secret Revelation of John, for example, translators need to know something about the cultural meaning of the words. And beyond these difficulties, the greatest translating challenge may come from the fact that the ensuing church traditions and doctrines have established a certain mindset that still distorts the intended message for modern readers.

Reading a text written in the second century requires a kind of vision that transcends most of what we've learned from the church over the millennia. What do these stories tell us—stories written before there was a canon of literature to defend; before there was a cathedral to pay for; before there was a church council to judge; before there was anything like a "Christian" center in Jerusalem, Rome, or Constantinople; and before Gregorian chants and Renaissance painters created our images of God? There is a Savior in the Secret Revelation of John, but he/she did not require a confession of creed to determine who is in or out.

The teacher who wrote the Secret Revelation of John was also aware that times had changed since Jesus had awakened so many hearts and minds over a century earlier. Jesus's spiritual call for awakening and transformation spoke to the hearts of his own generation, just as the people of second-century Alexandria experienced it in their time. Alexandria had been the heartbeat of the second century. Such luminaries as Philo, Basilides, Clement, Ptolemy (the philosopher), Galen, Valentinus, Justin, and Origen had all contributed in some measure to the explosive thinking, struggling, and learning in Alexandria. And the author of the Secret Revelation of John still had something new to say.

How do we make sense of it in the twenty-first century? Does it bring comfort and wisdom to those of us who live in a culture so extremely remote from its second-century origin? People today are more concerned about whether our grandchildren will survive a dramatic climate change, whether the world has enough space for the movement of refugees and emigrants, or what is in charge of the new world order. But true gems hold their value through the changing millennia, and the literary gems in the Secret Revelation of John convey an element of confidence and assurance we need especially now, when the pace of life is accelerating so rapidly.

The story of the Secret Revelation of John captures the hearts and minds of modern readers as well as it did those of second-century Alexandrians, because it opens with a picture most people relate to at some point in our human experiences. Jesus's disciple John (not the real person, but a character dramatizing the role) is distraught, struggling in the midst of a crisis of faith. Everything Jesus had taught him to love and believe in seemed to have gone up in smoke when Jesus was suddenly arrested, humiliated, and crucified by the Romans. Where was God? How did evil gain such power? Where would he (John) go next? What could he trust now?

The horror behind the questions was all too real in the second-century Mediterranean world. Twenty-first-century fears are not too different. What should we do when the fabric of global existence wears dangerously thin? Science and technology, politics and education have so far failed to reverse the threat. Strangely, our weakening faith in the promises of technology and biomedicine returns us to an equal footing with the ancient world before those promises ever appeared. We are glimpsing further evidence that our thoughts govern the health of our personal and corporate bodies more than technological wonders have ever been able to do.

Rome's endless military conquests exemplified the nature of power struggles. Emperors kept amassing greater power to bolster their hierarchical authority over the empire. Persons were captured and enslaved with every victory, women were raped, and thousands of dissenters (maybe like Jesus) were crucified. Women, poor people, and enslaved people—the majority of society—all served the preservation of power at the top. Everything and everyone had to remain and function within the proper order of hierarchical control.

Sadly, oppression still operates in almost every form of human society. Political extremism excites fear of disenfranchisement in new forms. The barbarity of pedophilia and sexual abuse is not yet erased from our modern world, and violence strikes indiscriminately.

When the Secret Revelation of John was written, there were signs that the Roman Empire was weakening. Could it sustain its expansion and hegemony into the future? As superpowers rearrange their relationships with each other and with other types of power on the world stage today, we still wonder where the power will come from and how it will be used.

Questions of health and of how people identified themselves as individuals in antiquity show up in the press and in scholarly inquiries today. But the questions arise for different reasons. Computer knowledge, from artificial intelligence to quantum-mechanics computers, threatens privacy and even our worth and identity. Do our minds belong to us or to computers, governments, or cyberspace criminals?

Illness plagues every society, ancient and modern. Our attitudes toward the body and the means of health are radically different from attitudes about health at the time of John's revelation. Even during the second century, ideas about health varied greatly. But the vision of healthcare that the Secret Revelation of John lays out is bold. Since the Savior rescues people from mental and bodily anguish, the Secret Revelation presents the idea of health itself as a state of thought. Salvation is not restricted to the sinful soul, but the Savior is a specialist in mind-comforting, mind-correcting, and mind-guiding. Therefore, people who respond to the Savior's teachings can ultimately learn how to avoid the thoughts of sin and sickness. The author of this revelatory message appeals to Jesus's style of healing-by-awakening rather than to the biomedical theories of antiquity, so his healing message resonates with people today who are thinking beyond the limitations of biotechnology.

The secret of John's revelation is that Jesus's teachings are available to meet cosmic and personal questions for all eras. The teachings are available, but they are secret—an ancient method of transmission. The teachings are secret, not just because they would offend some, but because they are hard to grasp. It requires more humility than intellectual depth, more sincerity than social prestige to understand them.

The ideas are abundantly available in the other texts in the Bible, but this second-century writer pulls them out of obscurity and defines them as the three essential explanations for healing and salvation. The book consists of three major parts, each one representing a major gem.

1. God is both loving and omnipotent good.

2. Evil is an impotent counterfeit or fraud.

3. The experience of healing is an essential element of full salvation for everyone.

The first gem—that God is both loving and omnipotent good—has entangled scholars and theologians for centuries. How could God be loving and let horrific things happen to people if God is really more powerful than evil forces? This is a brave author who tackles such a tough problem about God. The second gem is equally challenging: When every person on earth experiences evil as a reality, how could this author even *think* about evil as a mere fraud? But if this second gem is proven true, then it serves as a marvelous gift to the world. And, the third gem is probably more startling to church authorities than ordinary people. The idea that *everyone* has the opportunity to experience healing and being saved from evil forces rings true to those who are truly humble and sincere. Each gem first enters the human mind as a rough and worthless rock, but as the author of the Secret Revelation polishes them, one chapter at a time, they bring light, hope, and joy.

In the story's conclusion at the end of the Secret Revelation of John, the Savior tells John that he has "finished everything for you in your hearing" (Meyer, 132).[10] "The Savior communicated this to John for him to record and safeguard" (Meyer, 132).

10. The translations quoted in this book in a given context are chosen for how clearly they convey meaning in that context. The four most-quoted translations are (1) Davies, trans., *The Secret Book of John*; (2) King, *The Secret Revelation of John*; (3) Layton, *The*

Now, to open the pages of the book itself, imagine this Jewish teacher we met in Alexandria trying to make sense of the second-century upheaval he lived in. He imagines what Jesus might have said in a kind of post-resurrection scene to comfort his disciples in Jerusalem after his violent death, some 180 years before. The Alexandrian teacher envisions Jesus coming to his disciple John, who is distraught over the failure of the new movement, and Jesus opens John's eyes to a deeper understanding of the work of salvation. This is the story of the Secret Revelation of John.

Gnostic Scriptures, (4) Meyer, ed., *The Nag Hammadi Scriptusres*. They are to be abbreviated as King, Davies, Layton, and Meyer. For ease of locating references, I use book page numbers for Davies, Layton and Meyer, but chapter and verse for King. (There is no universal numbering system yet.)

2

The First Gem

God, the Power of Good

FIGURE 8

The title, The Apocryphon of John (Secret Revelation of John), follows the actual text in the upper part of this image. The text that directly follows this title is the Gospel of Thomas. This page is from the second book (codex) of the Nag Hammadi collection (Wikimedia Commons; image in the public domain).

The story begins with the spotlight on John, who is close to the breaking point. He and his brother James had left their father's business, given up everything, and for three years listened to every word Jesus uttered. His teachings and works confirmed all their Jewish hopes for peace and freedom from Roman domination.[1] Struggling to understand, to be faithful, and to confront his own fears and doubts, John was ready to give his all to this man.

But then suddenly Jesus was captured, and then brutally crucified!

Where to turn? Too many unanswered questions remain, and now there is only silence. In his distress, John heads to the temple, hoping to find a wise rabbi to talk to, or perhaps even to find comfort. He no sooner enters the gate, when a well-known Pharisee in Jerusalem, Arimanios by name, approaches, taunting him.

> Where is your teacher, the man that you used to follow? . . .
> And he (John) said to him, "He has returned to the place from which he came." The Pharisee said to him, "That Nazarene has greatly misled you, filled your ears with lies, closed your heart[s], and turned you away from the traditions of your ancestors." (Layton, 28)

This sort of ridicule is exactly what John had been afraid of. Turning from the temple, he heads straight for the mountain. He is alone with his thoughts, and the burning questions resurface:

> How indeed was the savior[2] chosen?
> And why was he sent into the world by his parent who sent him?
> And who is his parent who sent him?
> And what is that realm like, to which we shall go?
> . . . He did not tell us what that other [realm] is like. (Layton, 28)

Even more frightening than John's prospects of living with no answers, right at the moment of greatest despair, "the heavens opened" (Layton, 28)!

---

1. *Domination*, a term often used to define colonialism and chauvinism, refers to the belief in superiority that entitles the superior to the use of force to dominate others. Scott's *Domination and the Arts of Resistance* is a frequent reference for a description of the phenomenon and its practice in various societies.

2. Should *savior* be capitalized? Some translators, such as Layton, do not think so. Others, such as King and Meyer do think so. There is no capitalization in the Coptic version, so English translators must choose. On the one hand, the Savior usually does refer to a specific person, understood to be Jesus. On the other hand, the identity of the savior migrates from one person or entity to another. Because of the fluid identity of this saving presence in the text, I choose to capitalize *Savior* when the text seems to imply Jesus most nearly. And I choose to refer to the generic *savior* when the role of saving is the predominant idea associated with this character.

The whole world shone with a light. And within the light, a child appeared. John tries to get a better look, but the "child" becomes more like an elderly person. But then he changes again, looking more like a young man-servant. Doubting what he sees, John hears more clearly a calm, strong voice:

> John, John, why do you have doubts, and why are you afraid? . . .
> It is I who am with you [pl.] always.
> It is I who am the father
> It is I who am the mother
> It is I who am the son.[3]

> Now I have come to teach you (sing.) what exists, and what has come to be, and what must come to be, so that you might know about the invisible realm . . .; and to teach you about the perfect human being . . . so that you too might convey it to those who are like you in spirit, and who are from the immovable race of the perfect human being . . . so that they might understand . . . (Layton, 29)

John hardly even knew the right questions to ask. "What is that realm like?" The Savior comes in a vision to answer this question. But, according to the Savior, to comprehend the answer, John also needs to learn what it means to be a perfect human being. He will have to realize it in the depth of his being, not as a mere intellectual exercise. Being entrusted with these answers, he is also being prepared to convey them to others. Anyone who wants to understand will participate in the process of transformation. This author is preparing his readers so that they, too, will be able to participate in the process of learning if they are to understand the lessons he is about to teach.

The rest of the Secret Revelation of John is the author's comforting message in the form of a revelation from the savior to the anguished disciple. He—"the Savior," "Jesus," or "messenger from the divine"—prepares to teach John how creation all began, where evil came from, and how the savior works to restore the perfect harmony. This teaching will change his life.

---

3. An identity that blends generations, gender, and space (being "with you") is common in several ancient texts. It not only serves as an inclusive way of speaking, but also indicates a focus on the idea or function of the identity, rather than fixed personhood.

THE MAGNIFICENT REALM

According to the author of the Secret Revelation of John (using the voice of the Savior), creation itself is magnificent, and we need a clear picture of its goodness in order to understand both our origins and the answers to life's problems. God—who is kind of a blend of Father, Mother, and Son (Meyer, 111)—has established the divine realm through the supreme and infinite source of being and declares absolute authority. This *One* being is immaterial, both young and old. It/He/She is too great to be fully expressed by any human mind, but we can say that this One is complete, perfect, eternal, and unlimited in every way.

> It exists as the God and Father of the All, the invisible which dwells above the All, . . . imperishableness . . . It alone is eternal since It does not need anything. For It is totally perfect . . . It cannot be limited because there is nothing before It to limit It. . . . It is immeasurable because there is nothing which exists before It to measure It. (King, 4:3–15)

Imagine this immaterial God occupying both the center and circumference of all being. There is nothing greater, more powerful, or more beneficent. This idea is almost incomprehensible in human experience, because humans experience tragedy. We usually refrain from imagining a God who would be fully good and also all-powerful, because, if it were true, then we have to ask: where is God in our suffering? Is this God in an unreachable realm, completely irrelevant to human experience?

Standing before the scoffing of the whole world, this author bravely affirms the combination of God's goodness and all-power, while still maintaining the link to humanity. All human experience hinges upon a relationship with this God, and the Secret Revelation of John defends this most extraordinary claim of God's power of goodness. The savior's teaching is a gem. It calms fears and doubts, because the perfect God is able to provide a perfect realm for humanity. It also heals and saves.

It should not surprise us, though, that this gem-solution to the perennial suffering of humankind would have to stretch our minds in some way. This author challenges his readers to follow the logic of all-power and goodness in the context of human experience. The path to God's realm, he explains, is an interior one, and the first step is achieved through humility:

We would not know what is ineffable, we would not understand what is immeasurable, were it not for the one who has come from the Father. (Meyer, 109)

Readers are forewarned: to grasp the nature of God's power of goodness, they must admit that the knowledge of God's nature will not come from human senses, experience, or education. It will appear in human thought only from the Father (God). This first step—admitting the limitations of our own minds—may be the most difficult and the reason most people do not bother to try to know the Father's power or goodness. It is probably also the reason this good news remains a secret. But by yielding our own desire to control, we gain God's control through this knowledge of God's nature and goodness: this knowledge is called *gnosis*.

WHAT IS GNOSIS?

Gnosis isn't easily translated into English, so it's difficult to say what it is. But we know what it does. It brings about a satisfying awareness of where we have come from and where we're going.

It is a Greek word and is often translated as "knowledge," but that misses the uplifting and healing connotation. You don't get *gnosis*, for example, from a teacher or a well-rounded education, because everyone has it. God gives it to everyone. You also don't get it through a superior birthright, since it comes from God and not heredity or inheritance. It is the power of God expressed, and it results in a deeper understanding of God.

It could be the means of seeing beyond human perception and discerning a bigger picture of reality as the Mind/God perceives it. From that perspective, this knowledge protects people from the supposed powers of evil forces. Demons were always around. But with *gnosis*, people could feel protected from the demons' seductive powers of manipulation. They would be alert to the tricky and deceitful means employed by demons to cause forgetfulness, or even the loss of *gnosis*.

In a way, *gnosis* was like the magicians' tools for healing. For magicians and spiritual healers alike, the knowledge of a demon's name or its functions empowered the "knower" (*gnostic*) to banish demons. That is, *gnosis* empowered healers to restore health and freedom.

The next step is gaining an understanding and appreciation of stillness. Modern readers are usually unfamiliar with the well-known ancient phrase "unshakable generation," but it created an essential image of the divine realm in antiquity. In the Secret Revelation of John, the savior told John that he was to convey what he was to about to hear to those "who are from the unshakable generation of the perfect human" (Meyer, 108).

WHAT IS THE "UNSHAKABLE GENERATION"?

Like many of the now enigmatic phrases in the Secret Revelation of John, the idea of an "unshakable generation" (sometimes translated "immovable race" or "immovable generation") was well established in the first couple of centuries CE. It depicts the ideal and perfect realm inhabited by people who are unshakable or emotionally grounded. This is the *root* to which saved human beings will return. Today, we might think of it as a kind of spiritual calm that is present among those who have come to understand the meaning of the kingdom of God now and forever. The Savior urges those who are being rescued to

> Arise and remember that you are the one who has heard, and follow your *root*,[4] which is I, the compassionate. (King, 26:28, 29)

Also, in the Gospel of Mary,[5] the Savior explains to his disciples that every creature will dissolve again into their own proper root (2:3). Or, we might more readily recognize our roots in the words of the wizard Albus Dumbledore to the student Harry Potter: "It's our choices, Harry, that show what we truly are, far more than our abilities."[6] Knowing our roots reveals "the compassionate" and the calm assurance of our worth.

In the second century, the phrase "unshakable generation" circulated through a much wider audience than any specific religious community or sociological type.[7] Even as far back as the writing of the Psalms, the stillness of Yahweh was desirable. In Psalm 21:7 (NRSV[8]), the "king trusts in

---

4. There are no italicized words in Coptic, so all the italicized words in the quotes throughout this book are words that I have chosen to emphasize.

5. The Gospel of Mary is another important extracanonical text that may have been written around the time that the Secret Revelation of John was written.

6. Harry Potter Wiki, https://harrypotter.fandom.com/wiki/Albus_Dumbledore/.

7. Williams, *Immovable Race*, 6–7.

8. NRSV is the standard abbreviation for New Revised Standard Version, an English

the LORD, and through the *steadfast* love of the Most High he *shall not be moved*."

It also appears in the New Testament among later thinkers. The author of 2 Thessalonians urges his readers "not to be quickly shaken in mind or alarmed either by spirit or by word or by letter" (2:2 NRSV). Even later, Plotinus, a third-century writer, described it as an expression of "stability which accompanies conformity to the condition of the intelligible realm."[9]

Stillness was the great reward for spiritual maturity. Weaker characters were too susceptible to the damage caused by passions and emotional agitation. They had no resources for fending off the demons who had the power to cause agitating passions. Everybody—Jews, Greeks, Christ-followers, rich, and poor—knew that demons were the worst of enemies precisely because they instilled passions that resulted in disease and destruction! When the perfect stillness was broken, a believer's path to health and heaven could be blocked.[10]

STILLNESS

When I was little, my Sunday school teacher tried to describe heaven, explaining to our class that in heaven everything would be calm and perfectly in order. The image was terrifying to me: girls sitting quietly in polished living rooms wearing dresses, gloves, and hats. No running! No climbing trees (or falling out of them)! I secretly wept at the thought of being too good and having to end up in heaven someday, perhaps only being able to move by rocking in a rocking chair. At the time, I had no idea how much spiritual reckoning would lie ahead in order to attain such a reward!

Sometime later the value of stillness began to dawn on me. A calm approach to tense situations allows wisdom to prevail. Athletes who master high-speed action attain their precision though mental stillness. Stillness is neither boring nor inactive. It merely replaces mindless human reactions with constructive acts of mercy, precision, or wisdom.

One of the common translations of the term "unshakable generation"—"immovable race"—could make us wonder if there are racist threads woven

---

translation of the Holy Bible. This abbreviation is used throughout this book.

9. Quoted in Williams, *Immovable Race*, 16.

10. Williams, *Immovable Race*, 30.

into this heavenly realm. Who would be the people of this "generation" or "race"? The modern notion of *race* did not exist in antiquity, but the author of the Secret Revelation of John did think of his audience as defined in a special way, with boundaries. This "generation" or "race" (neither word a perfect translation) consisted of those who either were willing or ready to hear the spiritual ideas. The difference between those who heard and those who did not was real, but this distinction was a choice between thoughts rather than a predetermined type of racial or genetic separation. Controlling passions (thoughts) was the key to living in the realm of God's order, the original state of harmony and stillness.

WHERE DID THIS UNSHAKABLE GENERATION COME FROM? WHEN DID IT HAPPEN?

How did this unshakable group of people (this "race" or "generation") get started? The Secret Revelation of John presents a surprising response to the age-old debate over whether the earth was created within the past several thousand years or over millions of years. It resets the stage entirely through a closer look at the work of God—understood as timeless Spirit or Mind.

Knowing the resistance of the human mind to admitting what is beyond its own perception, the author of the Secret Revelation of John continues to reframe the story, insisting that the immeasurable things (beyond time and space) must begin with what God knows:

> For we do not understand these ineffable matters, and none of us knows those immeasurable things except for the one who appeared from the Father. This is the one who spoke to us alone. (King, 5:6, 7)

We might find ourselves pushing back against the modern attempts to understand the agelessness—or timelessness—of God's realm because our habits of depending on Newtonian physics kick in. But the author of the Secret Revelation of John insists that time is contradictory to the infinitude of the divine being.

> Time was not allotted to it [the One], since it receives nothing from anyone: what would be received would be on loan. (Meyer, 109)

The readers of this text are not being asked to accept ignorance of God, but to *know* God through means beyond the human habits of thought. The concept of time is not natural to the origin of being. That is a human convenience that distracts us from the fuller understanding.

THE PROBLEM WITH TIME

Some modern thinkers imagine life without the constraints of time. As recently as 2014, Bruce Grierson of the *New York Times* explored the topic of human experience of timelessness in an article titled, "What if Age Is Nothing but a Mind-Set?"[11] He reports on an experiment devised by Ellen Langer, in which men were tested after five days in an environment where they were treated as though they were decades younger. They were told not merely to reminisce about earlier times, but to "make a psychological attempt to *be* the person they were 22 years ago." At the end of the experiment, the men were suppler, showed greater manual dexterity, sat taller, and even their sight improved. They felt and looked younger. They put their minds in an earlier time, and "their bodies went along for the ride . . . The results were almost too good."

This experiment is a modern example of returning to one's roots, defying the tyranny of time and reinstating the true origin of creation.

So, dropping our measurements of time, we can discern how

> its eternal realm is incorruptible, at peace, dwelling in silence, at rest, before everything. (Meyer, 109)

Therefore, to better understand creation the way God reveals it, we should use the present tense: "How *does* creation come about?" Since God does not operate in a temporal way, through time or space, we replace the time-and-space spectrum with how and why it came about. The Secret Revelation of John explains:

> He (Mind/God) reflects on his image everywhere, sees it in the spring of the Spirit, and becomes enamored of his luminous water for his image is in the spring of pure luminous water surrounding him. His thought became a reality (Meyer, 110).

The thinking of the divine Spirit/Mind becomes the thing created. This concept is worth pondering before moving on to the effects of the creative phenomenon. This is not magic or a flight of fancy. If there is indeed a God with infinite power of goodness, then its process of creating is more *real*

11. Grierson, "What if Age Is Nothing but a Mind-Set?"

than the creation of a limited, troubled mortal unlike its own Self. John is being told that the Creator God/Mind has caused all being to exist through the action of thoughts. This thought-produced creation is us—human beings! We are reflections of the Mind who is enamored with us.

Creation is a thought-action that never functions within finite dimensions but with the purpose of loving its own idea. This Mind (God), which is neither corporeal nor confined to a single gender, *reflects* ("gazes") and creates by the act of thinking. There is no process of procreation that depends on bodies and on both male and female genders. If you're like me, you may need to stop and read those last two sentences again. Maybe ten more times.

REFLECTION AND IMAGE

In common usage, the English term *reflection* conveys two distinct meanings: (1) a serious thought and (2) throwing back an image without absorbing it. But for the author of the Secret Revelation of John, both concepts combine to express oneness in the relationship between Creator and creation. The Creator-Mind *thinks*, giving serious thought, and we, the thought of Mind, reflect back the image of the original (without absorbing it).

The logic may seem sound. We think a thought, and the thought should reflect what we're thinking. But in the life of human beings, this kind of relationship with God delivers a strong rebuke to our fragile egos. It is comforting to envision a God who is good and knows the goodness beyond what we imagine. But by being God's *reflection*—or as Genesis 1 has it, being the "image and likeness" of God—we are God's thoughts. Whether we think we have become great by our own creative powers or made a wreck of our lives, this text is telling us to look again. We have no inherent power to become anything greater or lesser than the goodness of God's image.

One hot summer day when my children were quite young, I was suffering mightily with a painful skin condition. I couldn't take my kids swimming and felt very sorry for myself. I remember bursting into tears of frustration and yelled at God: "How could you love such a wretched me?!"

In the silence that followed, I quieted down enough to hear a message that changed my life: "I don't love a wretched you. I love the *you* that I made."

I almost felt like some gentle hands touched my shoulders and turned me around, facing the opposite direction. I had been looking at everything backward. Instead of asserting the urgency and intensity of my feelings and my pain, I caught a glimpse of God as the cause. God didn't have to change anything; I was the one who needed to change. Admitting that God loved me the way God has *thought* me all along meant that I could rethink—or reflect back—what God was loving. Long story short, after a few months of thinking of myself differently, of what God must love of me, my agony lessened, my character softened, my skin returned to normal, and my kids went swimming.

Reflecting—with both meanings of the word—is a more peaceful way to live.

If you can succeed in removing yourself from the habit of depending on your physical senses as your sources of knowledge, then you can become more aware of the action of thoughts. And as you discern the timelessness of creation, you will also move forward on the path toward the power of goodness.

To be fair to those of us living with a worldview based on Newtonian physics, the notion of timeless creation may not have been as much of a stretch for ancient readers as it is for us today. They were more accustomed to the idea that when some disturbing event agitates the harmony of life, the solution lies in returning to the origin. In some ways, we do act out the same idea today too. When people discover they have taken the wrong route in a maze, they know to return to the beginning to find the right path. They don't carry the history of the mistake as they proceed toward the final goal. In ancient cultures, the repetition of acts that mirror the primordial awareness of creation serves to reset life's stage.[12]

The "Savior" in the Secret Revelation of John functions on this basis of timelessness. Within various shapes, genders, and methods, this Savior repeatedly corrects the evil acts of the fake god by returning the victim to his or her origin—the original way of being.

> It is she (the Savior) who aids the whole creation by toiling with him (the human), guiding him by correction toward his fullness, and teaching him about the descent of the seed and teaching him about the path of the ascent, the path which it had come down. (King, 18:24–27)

Returning to the original harmonious state of things is one of the rights of the "unshakable generation." It frees victims from the tyranny of time, because it acts as a reset. Whatever caused some form of agitation ceases its disturbance when people return to their original state. This return

---

12. Eliade offers many examples in *The Myth of the Eternal Return*, 76.

is no return to the "good old days" as everything was before; it is better characterized as a recognition that catches a glimpse of the creating God. A better discernment of it opens the path to greater freedom.

THE ALL-POWERFUL REALM OF GOODNESS

John had already been convinced of the goodness of his Master and his teaching. He knew it was "the immeasurable light, which is pure, holy, and unpolluted" (King, 4:20). It is free of passions and the tyranny of time. But defeat of his Master's mission at the hands of the Romans was an unbearable situation. Of what value is goodness without power? The Savior explains that, indeed, this realm is the source of *all* power. "The One (God-figure) is a *sovereign that has nothing over it*" (Meyer, 108; italics added).[13]

A common way for ancient writers to express the "nothing-else-ness" of God or God's incomparability to anything else was in a negative sense:

> It is more than divine, *without* anything existing over It. For *nothing* lords over It . . . It is *not* something among existing things, but It is far superior—not as being superior to others as though It is comparable to them, but as that which belongs to Itself. (King, 4:6, 29; italics added)

John will certainly have more questions later about how an all-powerful God could be possible, considering the failure he had recently witnessed at Jesus's crucifixion. But first the Savior insists that John must know the full extent of the goodness and power of the divine realm before he can fully comprehend how the Savior will rescue from evil powers. The author is also careful to note that the superior power of this divine being conveys no competitive one-upmanship with any other being. Its power is not used against its own created beings, but against the supposed powers of contradiction. As the story unfolds, we will see how this power is always used to *empower* the beloved beings in the divine realm.

To help his readers find themselves in the story, the author of the Secret Revelation of John employs a technique common to several ancient writers—the use of myth. It characterizes the nature of the important truth

13. The Berlin Codex (shorter) version of this verse is, "The Unity is a monarchy with nothing ruling over it" (King, 4:2). There are two basic versions of the Secret Revelation of John—commonly known as the longer and shorter versions. The Nag Hammadi Library contains two copies of the longer version and one copy of the shorter version. The shorter version is from a different source, commonly known as the Berlin Codex. It is sometimes helpful to compare the two versions to see if one helps to elucidate the other.

he strives to convey, and, enfolded within the larger story of salvation, it introduces characters and plots already familiar to second-century readers.

MYTHS ARE NOT FANTASY STORIES FOR GULLIBLE PEOPLE

Myths are not the same as fake news. We deplore being taken in by fake news and tricked into believing untruths. But myths are different. They provide a rationale for things when science, philosophy, or technology fail to help us.

People still look for answers to hard questions. Why do bad things happen to good people? What causes natural disasters? How would an earthquake be explained in antiquity? One answer might be that an angry god shook the earth. The idea was not meant to mislead, but to help listeners consider where the great powers might come from.

When people look to religion to answer questions, myths become useful vehicles of truth-explaining. Some myths are simply elaborate stories of fantasy, of course, but most myths express a truth for somebody. Cupid, for example, was the god of love in Roman mythology. He is (still) usually depicted as a winged child armed with a bow and arrow. His arrows could either draw people together or pull them apart. This is a myth that offers an explanation for why people can be so intensely drawn to each other and why other relationships can fail to evolve as one might hope.

In a religious context, myths put people in touch with sacred realities, pointing to the fundamental sources of being, power, and truth. They enable people to interpret their lives and find worth and purpose.

Like other stories, myths include characters, setting, conflict, plot, and resolution. No one needs to believe in a child with wings in order to understand that relationships can be intense and confusing. But Cupid's name, along with his role in influencing relationships, evokes a certain way to comprehend the intensity. Cupid can show up in comic strips, Valentine cards, songs, and daily conversation, acting out different scenarios but maintaining an identity understood in the popular culture.

The ancient characters in the Secret Revelation of John were well-known to its audience and also appear in a number of second-century texts. They may also have made appearances in songs and poems, because their mythical identities were known in that cultural setting. Frequently, ancient myths feature metamorphosis—a change in shape or form—so that a character fulfills multiple roles, and we will see examples of this in the Secret Revelation of John.

Barbelō, Yaldabaoth, Epinoia, Pronoia, Seth, and Sophia are some of the characters in the Secret Revelation of John who play important roles in the drama of the myth, but most of their names and identities are lost on modern readers. They can be complex, changing genders and identities. But second-century readers would have known them and caught the nuances of their character development, as they appeared in other widely circulated texts at the time.

Barbelō is closely associated with power, even though she plays a number of dual roles in the Secret Revelation of John. She represents both the subject and object of power, both cause and effect, and both the female counterpart to the Invisible Spirit as well as the *object* of the Invisible Spirit's creation.

By *asking* for foreknowledge, incorruptibility, Life, and Truth, and receiving them, she becomes the "perfect power." Power in this sense seems associated with both the effect of what Invisible Spirit does, as well as Barbelō's own power to cause. When the Father "looks into Barbelō" she conceives light, or good:

> She is *the power which is before the All* . . . she who is the *perfect power,* Barbelō, the perfect aeon of the glory. (King, 5:15, 20; italics added)[14]

> She [Barbelō, also Protennoia] *became the universal womb*, for she precedes everything, the Mother-Father, the first Human,[15] the holy Spirit, the triple male, *the triple power*, the androgynous one with three names . . . (Meyer, 110; italics added)

"Becoming a womb" implies the mothering birth or cause of other beings, and reference to the "triple power" is the closest language in this text resembling our modern sense of omnipotence, or all-power.

As strange as it may seem to modern logic, Barbelō conveys the sense of the most powerful—or the all-powerful—by both receiving and giving all power. But that dual action does not seem to lessen the sense

14. This quote is from the Berlin Codex (shorter version) translation. Codex II (longer version) reads: "She is the first power which is before them all . . . the first power, the glory of Barbelō, the glory which is perfect in the aeons." It is not clear whether the possibly redacted (longer) version implies that Barbelō is the *first among others*, or that the "first" is a superlative expression.

15. Some scholars translate the Coptic word *rōma* (often translated as *man* or *human*) as *Human* with a capital *H* because it indicates an identity above the ordinary human concept, and it is also not a reference to a male person.

of *omni*potence, because cause must have an effect, creator must have a relationship with its creation, love must love an object. Whatever consists of All-power must overpower anything that would oppose its capacity to *em*power its beloved creation.

The Savior, who is acting on behalf of the transcendent Being, comes to comfort John and brings assurance that every form of opposition will be met through the absolute authority of Spirit/Mind Creator. In the end, the Savior

> raised him up [the person suffering the effects of the counterfeit spirit's cruelty] and sealed him with the light of the water with five seals so that death would not have power over him from this day on. (King, 26:32–33)

The "five seals" (representing baptism) strengthen the soul in its battle against passions, the source of all human suffering.[16] Death is to be put down forever. As will become increasingly evident through the work of the Savior, the relationship between the invisible Spirit and humanity is retained as a thought-governing authority. Demons rule the passions, and passions manipulate emotions and thoughts, which, in turn, cause pain, suffering, and death. But the Spirit overrules the demons.

There is good reason, then, for the authority of the realm to be established through a thinker-thought relationship, as the chief of demons—the strongest enemy—will attempt to use mental trickery to oppose the divine dominance. Supreme power is expressed as omniscience, as Truth overruling falsity, and as Mind overcoming ignorance.

THE PERFECT HUMAN BEING

With the knowledge of God's power of goodness, John is now ready to learn about the perfect Human[17] being that the Savior promised to teach so that he can

---

16. King, *The Secret Revelation of John*, 149.

17. I adopt the system of some scholars who use capital *H* to distinguish between the perfect Human of the heavenly realm and the human constructed through a type of procreation. For example, King translates chapter 9, verse 2, in part: "the will of autogenes, the invisible Spirit named the perfect Human, the first revelation."

> convey it to those who are like you in spirit, and who are from the
> immovable race of the perfect human being . . . so that they might
> understand . . . (Layton, 29)

They ultimately come from the one Being (virgin Spirit, Mother, Father, Cause) who is intelligent and is meaningfully expressed. But John must understand the nature of the Father, the means of creation, and the means by which humans express the completeness of the one Being. Barbelō starts the action by asking for various essential elements to be present:

> Barbelō asked the Invisible Virgin Spirit to give her Foreknowledge, and the Spirit consented . . . She asked again to be given Incorruptibility . . . again to be given Life eternal . . . again to be given Truth. (Meyer, 110–11)

When the Father gazed into Barbelō, the only Child came forth, and this Child is also identified as an "aeon." These *aeons* are more like "states of thought" or "beings" than locations or measurable units of time. The Child is self-generated to perfection and sends forth four more lights, which also become *aeons*. These *aeons*, coming from the four lights, produce such characteristics as grace, memory, love, perfection, peace, and last of all— wisdom (*sophia*).

Then Human beings begin to appear in the same way that the Child came forth.

WHERE DO HUMANS COME FROM?

What parent hasn't struggled to find the right way to explain to their young children where babies come from? And yet even when those children are old enough to study the human reproductive system in school, we all know these studies don't fully answer the question either. Where did the baby's consciousness come from?

This is an important subject to the author of the Secret Revelation of John, because the identification of a human as God's own creation is central to his thesis that God is the only true cause, and nothing really exists outside the creative work of the perfect God.

The origin of consciousness is significant, because conscious thought may identify a person more profoundly than their physical traits. And it is more likely that consciousness derives from the one original Mind/Spirit than from mindless, inert matter. The expression for this act of creating by a Spirit/Mind in the Secret

Revelation of John is that the creative One "gazes," and the idea of the human appears. Another way to say it is that the Creative One thinks a thought, and the thought is made manifest.

Each person, therefore, is understood to be the result of the Creator thinking a thought. Before we reject this explanation for the origin of consciousness too quickly, let's take the temperature on contemporary thought about the origin of consciousness. A simple Google search yields thousands of results, with titles such as

"Why Can't the World's Greatest Minds Solve the Mystery of
   Consciousness?"

"Human Consciousness: Where Is It From and What Is It For?"

"Does Consciousness Pervade the Universe?"

"Where Does Consciousness Come From?"

If we have no evidence of consciousness originating in matter, then the notion of humanity's origin deriving from Mind ought to be taken seriously. The beauty of con-sciousness[18] is its implication that the experience of being conscious is a kind of knowing awareness with something: being aware of relationships. "With-ness" cannot occur in the past tense, but the Creator Mind creates con-sciousness only in the present tense.

Although the Secret Revelation of John had not yet been discovered at Nag Hammadi before the death of Mary Baker Eddy in 1910, she wrote in a strikingly similar manner about the creation of humankind. "Man"—meaning the ideal Human—is the "idea" of God. She wrote:

"Man": God's spiritual idea, individual, perfect, eternal.

"Idea": An image in Mind; the immediate object of
   understanding.—Webster[19]

Drawing on the logic of this syllogism, she asks, then "can there be any birth or death for man, the spiritual image and likeness of God?"[20]

On this basis, we can explain the conscious existence of humanity as the spiritual image and likeness of God. This existence is not contingent on the conditions of matter or of a material birth process.

Ultimately we may be asking if the identification of a person's origin in matter is more or less reliable than the identification of the person's origin in

18. Splitting the word emphasizes the Greek and Latin prefix con-, which signifies "with." This idea came to light in a private conversation with Arthur Dewey.

19. Eddy, Science and Health, 115.

20. Eddy, Science and Health, 206.

consciousness. In the Secret Revelation of John, the author argues that these two sources of one's identity appear to exist on opposite ends of a spectrum, and that the *psyche* (the soul) is able to slide more toward one end (consciousness) and less toward the other end (matter). But, the critical point of his argument is that the conscious identity is the only absolute reality, even though it is invisible to the senses. Whereas the physical senses arguing in favor of the material (unconscious) identity is false and obscures the limitless possibilities of the true Human.

When Humans appear as they are described in the Secret Revelation of John, the consciousness of memory, love, peace, and so forth, is already present. The first human, Adamas, who is the perfect and ideal, becomes the model for the counterfeit creator to try to copy. Three other categories of Humans represent varying degrees of closeness to the divine image.

FIGURE 9

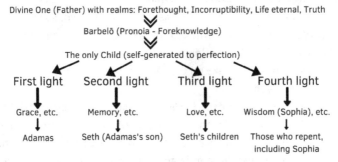

Simplified Structure of the Heavenly Realm

Divine One (Father) with realms: Forethought, Incorruptibility, Life eternal, Truth

Barbelō (Pronoia - Foreknowledge)

The only Child (self-generated to perfection)

First light   Second light   Third light   Fourth light

Grace, etc.   Memory, etc.   Love, etc.   Wisdom (Sophia), etc.

Adamas   Seth (Adamas's son)   Seth's children   Those who repent, including Sophia

Pronoia, triple formed: Ennoia (self-reflection), Pronoia (thought), Protennoia (Its thinking)

The actual text of the Secret Revelation of John is more complex than the diagram here. Even this simplified picture of the heavenly realm is rather mind-boggling to the modern Western imagination. Why so many characters, so many aeons, so many kinds of humans, so many relationships between creators and created, and all of them morphing into different characteristics? One reason might be due to the fact that in second-century Alexandria, Plato's popular book *Timaeus* appeared to offer more or different answers to the questions of creation than the Jews had offered with the myth in Genesis. The Secret Revelation uses characters and plot structure similar to the *Timaeus* to respond to the questions of the day, but it builds upon Genesis and directly contradicts Plato's teaching.

Sophia (Wisdom) is one of the aeons from the last of the four lights, and in a personified way, Wisdom (*Sophia*) is also well-known among second-century readers as Lady Wisdom. By the time the Secret Revelation of John was written, Sophia's character had taken on different roles throughout a long trajectory of Jewish, Greek, and early Christ movements. And even within the myth in the Secret Revelation of John, Sophia will take on several roles, sometimes even those that appear contradictory. But her identity as *wisdom* supplies theological depth and wit to the myth.

WHO IS SOPHIA?[21]

Sophia (the Greek word for "wisdom") is the most important but enigmatic character in the Secret Revelation of John. She comes into the story with a history that readers would have already known by the time this myth was written. So, a little backstory will help modern readers follow the twists and turns in the plot.

At least in some form, Sophia may be known as far back as the Hebrew Wisdom writings, where "wisdom" (*chokmah* in Hebrew) appears in Proverbs in a personified context. "Lady Wisdom," as she is later known, speaks in the first person: "I, Wisdom, . . . know where to discover knowledge and discernment" (8:12). She is not really a divine attribute of God or a distinct goddess on her own, even though she appears to take on the function of God or express God's active involvement in the world.

Probably at some other period, Wisdom's role in the Hebrew text, the Book of Wisdom, strongly resembles the saving acts of the well-known goddess Isis from earlier Near Eastern traditions. But this character particularly meets the need for Jews who had returned from exile and had been searching for a theological answer to the injustice and chaos in the world. Whether the Jews were influenced by Isis or not, Wisdom, according to Jewish writing, was present when God created the order of the world, and she is able to reassure humanity of the continued existence of this order.

Her relationship with God becomes increasingly intertwined (still in the Book of Wisdom). She sits on the throne of God and is loved by God. God creates all that exists through his Word (*Logos*); and by him (God), Wisdom forms humanity. She knows almost everything, controls everything, and renews all things.

---

21. For this overview of the historical development of the meaning of *Sophia*, I draw on Humble, *Sophia the Enigma*. The conclusions I draw for the Secret Revelation of John are my own.

Then either centuries later or only decades later—depending on whether the Wisdom of Solomon was written centuries before or rather close to the time of Jesus—a devout Jew and active Greek philosopher living in Alexandria named Philo wrestled with the meaning and role of Sophia/Wisdom and Logos. Although Logos had appeared in philosophical thought about three hundred years earlier than Sophia traditions, Logos and Sophia ran parallel in religious thought. They were both evidence of God's presence in the world.

But Philo, with his Hellenistic background, merged the two by placing Sophia in the upper realm of the divine and replacing her active role in the world with Logos. Philo extends Sophia's loving relationship with God, portraying her as the bride, wife, and lover to God and mother of both creation and Logos. Having established God as the Father, and Wisdom as the Mother of Logos, he identifies Logos as the "first-born of God," "the image of God," and the "second God."[22]

Paul perpetuates the role of Sophia but replaces her with Jesus Christ. Jesus now becomes the agent both in creation and reconciliation, the intermediary between God and humanity. In Philippians, for example, Jesus was first in the form of God and later took the form of human, the role earlier ascribed to Sophia.

In Q and the Gospels of the New Testament, Sophia's relationship with Jesus fluctuates.[23] In several Q passages, Jesus appears as if he is Sophia's son and final prophet.[24] In Matthew and Luke, though, Sophia is the primary source of Jesus's revelation and wisdom. In fact, in Matthew, Jesus is presented as Wisdom herself.[25]

In a number of Christian-related texts excluded from the canon, such as the Secret Revelation of John, Sophia's relationship with the world becomes increasingly complex. Often grouped in different schools of thought,[26] most of these texts develop Sophia's role as explanation or pattern for humanity's fall and subsequent suffering, repentance, and redemption. But the widely different texts

---

22. Schnackenburg, *Gospel according to John*, 486.

23. The Gospels of Matthew and Luke share some strikingly similar passages that many scholars assume to have come from another source, commonly called Q.

24. Johnson-DeBaufre explains why these passages in Matthew and Luke imply that Jesus could be considered a son of Sophia, in Johnson-DeBaufre, *Jesus among Her Children*, 44–45, 56–62.

25. Suggs, *Wisdom, Christology, and Law in Matthew's Gospel*, 28. Also, for further discussion on the relationship between Jesus and Sophia in the Gospel of Matthew, see Dunn, *Christology in the Making*.

26. Two such schools of thought are frequently categorized by scholars as "Valentinian" or "Sethian." Valentinus was a well-known early second-century theologian whose works emphasized the pursuit of *gnosis*. Seth, the third son of Adam and Eve, was thought by several second-century authors to be the heavenly savior.

represent different motives and philosophical perspectives on the sins and suffering of humanity and humanity's reunification with the divine realm.

In the Secret Revelation of John, Sophia follows these traditions: She expresses God's active involvement in the world; as consort of Infinite Spirit, she is like a bride or wife; she acts as the agent in both creation and reconciliation; and she renews all things; she was present when God created the order of the world, so she is able to reassure humanity of the continued existence of this order.

Now that the relationship between all these categories of people—Adam, his son Seth, Seth's children, and those who repent—is settled, the author of the Secret Revelation of John reminds us that we all have the same purpose. We live to glorify the Spirit that caused us to be:

> These are the creatures that glorify the Invisible Spirit. (Layton, 114)

He will explain later how it is that *everyone* is included in these categories. But for now, we readers are asked to cherish this gem. Note that it represents the permanent reality of the beauty, perfection, and promise of God's power of goodness. All of us as Humans are created as the thoughts of God, held together as the unshakable generation. The Secret Revelation of John has made clear in many ways that there is *no* power that can disrupt this perpetual goodness. And the concluding point is that we exist to glorify this wondrous God.

Before the author can move on to feature the dazzling wonder of the second gem, we readers must be thoroughly convinced and at peace with the fullness, goodness, truth of God's realm. Without this conviction, the second gem will remain encrusted with layers of doubt and fear.

3

The Second Gem
Evil Exposed as a Fraud

How many ways can you say that God is all-powerful and good? Apparently, the author of the Secret Revelation of John looked at this gem through the lens of a kaleidoscope and explained its dazzling relevance from countless angles. About one-third of the book is devoted to making certain his readers would be convinced of the reality and power of this God, this Goodness. It makes sense that our author would have to lay such a deep and firm foundation for this, because the winds of doubt are fierce, shaking the faith of nearly every human being. The unshakable generation will need to withstand the arguments of every form of evil imaginable.

This second gem, or the second third of the book, is precious beyond words, because it gives to humans the authority to resist evil in all its cruel and forceful methods. And it all hinges on Sophia.

Remember that in the second century almost everyone was familiar with the personified Wisdom (*Sophia*) from Proverbs and many other sources, and knew that Lady Wisdom was conceived as a savior with a deeply intertwined relationship with God, who loves her. Paul perpetuates this role for Sophia but replaces her with Christ Jesus, who now becomes the intermediary between God and humanity. The author of the Secret Revelation of John merges both ideas, to an extent. First, there's Jesus, who does come to humanity—as in the beginning of the story—when he suddenly appears to help John. And then Sophia appears, taking on the tragic role of acting out the human experience of sin for the sake of the sinful humans she has come to guide out of their suffering. Although she knows that she is the object of God's love, and as a partner of Infinite Spirit, she displays the nature of sin and evil so that all of God's children can learn from her how to return to their roots in God's realm.

Paul conceived of Christ Jesus, also of the divine realm, as taking on full humanhood. Christ Jesus

> emptied himself, taking the form of a slave, being born in human likeness. And being found in human form, he humbled himself and became obedient to the point of death—even death on a cross. (Phil 2:7, 8 NRSV)

In a parallel move, Sophia also takes on a role of human-likeness in the Secret Revelation of John, contrary to her wise nature. Her specific human-like behavior was *willing* something besides the will or consent of her male partner, Infinite Spirit. She took on the form of an ego, of a mind apart from the divine.

> She wanted to bring forth something like herself, without the consent of the Spirit, who had not given approval, without her partner and without his consideration . . . She did not find her partner, and she considered this without the Spirit's consent and without the knowledge of her partner. (Meyer, 114–15)

Sophia (Wisdom) takes on the most *unwise* thing to do, because the entire order of divine realm is based on the *syzygy*—or male-female pairing—where both male and female thoughts commingle and produce offspring. Fortunately, for the sake of the story's conclusion, Sophia is precisely the perfect character for this role, because only Wisdom is able to untangle the confusion that ensues due to the disconnect from God's original order. Sophia chooses alienation for the sake of loving union.

She knows intimately what went wrong and how to repair it. For this reason, she is the one called upon to take on human sinfulness in order to save the humans from their sinfulness. Coming from the complete and unshakable realm, she can demonstrate repentance and the way back to the original source of being.

As we look more deeply into the consequences of a will apart from God, we will appreciate why it was necessary to establish the depth and authority of the perfect, unshakable realm in the first place. The savior's job is to awaken and remind sufferers and sinners of their roots, their home in peaceful unity with God.

THE ORIGIN OF EVIL

A tragedy greater than anyone could have imagined occurred with Sophia's desire. Her willful desire came to be, and her offspring of disobedience and ignorance appeared:

> When Sophia saw what her desire had produced, it changed into the figure of a snake with the face of a lion. Its eyes were like flashing bolts of lightning. She cast it away from her, outside that realm so that none of the immortals would see it. She had produced it ignorantly. (Meyer, 115)

FIGURE 10

Yaldabaoth, the Chief Ruler: "a lion-faced deity found on a Gnostic gem in Bernard de Montfaucon's *L'antiquité expliquée et représentée en figures* (1722). It may be a depiction of the Demiurge" (image [in the public domain] and description courtesy of Wikipedia).

Readers of the Secret Revelation of John are now introduced to the work-ings of evil itself. Sophia has named this horrifying offspring Yaldabaoth (whose name scholars of today do not understand), and she became in-creasingly agitated as the extent of his evil powers revealed itself to her.

Taking power from his mother, Yaldabaoth decides to create entirely on his own. Not just an offspring, but a whole realm of evil forces! In a parody on his mother's disconnect from her partner, Yaldabaoth unites with the mindlessness within himself to produce his own world. (Note this little clue here, for future reference: that his creating partner is "mindless-ness"—quite a contrast to *wisdom*.) His first order of business in his top-down creation includes a dozen ruling authorities. The first seven are kings who reign over the seven heavens (including the sun, moon, and known planets), and the last five reign over the depth of the abyss (Hades).

Yaldabaoth dwells in darkness, so he shares some of the fire from his eyes with his authorities. But when darkness mixes with the light, they dwell in gloom thereafter. There is wickedness in this gloomy atmosphere, because Yaldabaoth proclaims: "I am God and there is no other god beside me!" (Meyer, 116). Any reader of Moses's books of the law, either in antiq-uity or today, would recognize the blasphemy spewing from the mouth of Yaldabaoth, where he directly defies the God of Israel. This God had said many centuries before, "I am the Lord your God . . . you shall have no other gods before me" (Exodus 20:2–3 NRSV).

Full of determination to garner all power over his whole creation, Yaldabaoth proceeds with his vision of absolute control over his creation.

> The rulers each created seven powers for themselves, and the powers each created six angels until there were 365 angels. (Meyer, 116)

There are now enough of these "angels"—messages sent from their god—to manipulate each day of the year. Since we already know the evil intent of Yaldabaoth, we can easily discern the evil forces behind the angels. We might think of Yaldabaoth's angels as we would think of demons or evil spirits today, rather than as sweet voices of goodness.

The author of the Secret Revelation of John explains:

> They were named after the glory above for the destruction of the powers. Although the names given them by their maker were powerful, the names given them after the glory above would bring about their destruction and loss of power. (Meyer, 117)

My paraphrase of this section may clarify the motives of the Chief Demon:

> [Yaldabaoth] still wants to put some of the glory that belongs to heaven into the grasp of each of his authorities/powers. He conceives of various combinations, and they come to pass. For example, he pairs goodness with the first authority, Althouth (the sheep's face). Forethought, divinity, lordship, kingship, zeal, and intelligence are paired up with the others.
>
> Why? Not to give them hope for a good future, but for the purpose of destroying them. It's their dual nature that will ultimately do them in. Jealousy energizes Yaldabaoth's plan for his own creation. He will make it *appear* just like the original divine creation, in the same indestructible pattern.[1]

Here is another one of many clues we will continue to watch for as Yaldabaoth exposes his evil nature. First, we noted that he mated with mindlessness. Now, although he never lived in or witnessed the glory above—or the place his mother came from—he is competing for power against this God above. He takes the names from this glory above because of their power, and he gives them to each of his angels. What he does not know is that those are the very names that will ultimately bring about their destruction and loss of power. Evil destroys itself.

But until that happens, we humans will search for further clues until we are convinced of the falsity, or fraudulence, of evil. We begin to understand why the first gem—the goodness and all-power of God—was so essential to our future. As these mighty forces of evil appear so real, so powerful, and so present, we watch carefully the process of creation to distinguish the difference between the completed creation of the perfect God and agitation stirred up by Yaldabaoth.

ESCAPE ROOMS

If you've had a chance to work your way out of one of the popular Escape Rooms now dotting many major cities, you'll know what it's like to look for clues that guide you to the next bit of information leading to your escape. When you first step in, with the door closing behind you, everything in the room appears quite normal. You see no hints at the solution to your problem.

---

1. This passage is from the full paraphrase in Chapter 6 in this book. See page 116 for this passage in chapter 13.

And then you start thinking. You know that when you entered the room, it was designed for you to discover the way out. As you admit the possibilities, you begin to notice things little by little. It doesn't all add up at first, but you take in one small detail at a time, and after a while, the tiny fragments come together to form some kind of key to unlock a significant step forward.

Escaping the mystery of evil in the Secret Revelation of John works similarly. At first it seems quite normal that evil is real, powerful, and present. But this is part of the guise intended to throw you off. If you don't think beyond the appearances, you'll remain in the realm of evil forces just as certainly as you would be stuck in the pretend "escape room." Maintaining your conviction that there really is a solution inspires you to keep trying, even when the evidence is so slim.

The value of the second gem of the Secret Revelation of John lies in its promise that there is a solution to the problem of evil, even when the evidence of the first gem fades into a distant darkness in our human experience.

THE POWER OF SOPHIA'S REPENTANCE

No sooner did Yaldabaoth complete his order of power with his 365 minions, but his mother Sophia

> began to move around. She realized that she was lacking something when the brightness of her light diminished. She grew dim because her partner had not collaborated with her.
>
> I [John] said, "Lord, what does it mean that she moved around?" [The Lord replies:] "She did not dare to return, but she was agitated. This agitation is the moving around." (Meyer, 117)

More clues to the nature of evil begin to emerge as Sophia discerns the evidence of her son's blasphemy and arrogance. First, with Yaldabaoth taking his mother's light and power, she recognizes the darkness and its source in her disobedience to the law of partnership. Her agitation marks the telltale sign that she dwells among the humans who have not found their way to the "unshakable generation."

> When the Mother realized that the trappings of darkness had come into being imperfectly, she understood that her partner had not collaborated with her. She repented with many tears. The whole realm of Fullness heard her prayer of repentance and offered praise on her behalf to the Invisible Virgin Spirit, and the

Spirit consented . . . She was to remain in the ninth heaven until she restored what was lacking in herself. (Meyer, 118)

In Sophia's prayer of repentance expressed "with many tears," we have found another significant clue that unlocks one of the mysteries of evil. Repentance is a necessary step required for salvation, and it involves an honest recognition of the temptation of evil. Sophia recognizes and admits her mistake. Her tears indicate her sincere desire to turn around and to live in compliance with the order established in the realm of the unshakable generation. By following her example of repentance, we (readers of the Secret Revelation of John) are able to discern where humanity has moved off track and how the restoration will take place. The picture of humanity, as conceived by Yaldabaoth, comes into clearer focus.

What Are We Made Of?

We will need to remember that creation is fully complete, even as it is always happening. Whatever continues to evolve is an expression of this perfect completeness, but nothing new can mar the fullness and perfection of creation. However Yaldabaoth, who is ignorant, arrogant, and powerless, tries to mock the one God and creation by creating on his own. Why would we care about the creation produced by a mindless monster? Precisely because the object of this creation is the one that we humans tend to believe the most! It tempts us to trust our feelings more than our understanding. Sophia's model of repentance helps us to see the mistakes that result from trusting our feelings above the truth and to turn from them. But we must be willing and ready to discern these flaws. As we continue to search for the clues that rescue us from pain, we will come to realize that our feelings have been manipulated. We'll see why we feel so much like the creation as Yaldabaoth formed it.

Yaldabaoth said to the authorities with him, "Come, let's create a human being after the image of God and with the likeness to ourselves, so that this human image may give us light." (Meyer, 119)

Alarm bells should be ringing when we hear these plans spill from the mouth of Yaldabaoth. We are to be created in the *image* of God. That has already taken place! But then that image will become *like* this monster? And then *we* are expected to give light to this new god-monster? This is preposterous, but it does provide another clue.

47

There are times, indeed, when we feel the joy of glorifying the God in heaven above as that God's image. But we all know the other times when we feel like monsters ourselves. Why did we behave so badly? Why do we feel such ambivalence between our own goodness and sinfulness? Why do we find so many of our prayers taking the form of offering the one God some light for what we think He/She does *not* know? Now we know that our *feelings* inform us that we are the creation of Yaldabaoth. But we will hold to that first gem (the knowledge of God who is good and omnipotent) while we acknowledge the weak testimony of our own senses.

Now we will witness Yaldabaoth's supposed creative act.

YALDABAOTH'S CREATION OF PEOPLE

Yaldabaoth told the authorities to join him in the creation of a human being according to the image of God and likeness to themselves.

> They created through their respective powers, according to the features that were given. Each of the authorities contributed a psychical feature corresponding to the figure of the image they had seen. (Meyer, 119)

My paraphrase of this verse amplifies what Yaldabaoth and his subordinate authorities were up to:

> In a fit of jealousy, Yaldabaoth coaxes his subordinate demons, "Come on, let's create a human according to the image of God, but in *our* likeness! This way, the light from the image will illuminate *us*."
>
> So in full compliance with his will, the demons/angels begin to create. Using each other's powers, according to the characteristics given to them, all the demons collaborate on creating a human being. Each demonic authority contributes to the human's psyche some characteristic corresponding to the model of the image they had seen of God. The psyche, sometimes called soul, is the in-between place, between the naturally inanimate powers of the demons and the invisible Spirit. A person might be inclined either toward the image of God or toward the likeness of the demons at any time.[2]

2. This passage is from chapter 15 of the full paraphrase in Chapter 6 of this book.

THE PSYCHICAL PART OF US

In the modern world, we may be more familiar with psychic powers that seem to act outside of natural law. Or, we may consider people with special powers of telepathy or clairvoyance to be *psychic*.

But in antiquity, the term *psychic* carried a more natural connotation. In the Bible we read of Paul distinguishing between spiritual, *psychic,* and fleshly people (See 1 Corinthians 2:13–31). If you read multiple English translations of 1 Corinthians 2:14, you'll see that there is no easy way to translate the Greek term *psychical* today. Some refer to it as the "natural man" and others as "unspiritual"; others don't bother to try a translation. They lose the distinction between *psychical* and *spiritual*, and simply call it "spiritual."

But this third aspect of humanhood is critical to an understanding of the world of Yaldabaoth and of why Yaldabaoth's psychic creation feels like our own human experience. Paul and others use these three elements to indicate the relationship between humans and the divine on a scale beginning with spiritual reality and ending with the darkness of materiality, the fleshly aspect of a person. The spiritual is the original perfection that endures forever and is wholly good. The material, fleshly element is mindless and always leads to self-destruction.

Between the material and the spiritual, the psychical element corresponds to what feels most like the human experience. The psyche can experience varying amounts of light and dark, joy and sorrow, good and evil. The *psyche* is the soul, which can relate to either the guidance of the divine Mind or the demons, who manipulate the feelings, or passions. What's dangerous about the psyche is that the psyche can lead humans to think their *feelings* are more real than the knowledge given to them in the beginning by God. The psyche can make them *forget* their original perfection and goodness, even though the original is still present and true. We can too easily identify with the material sense of things and fall into dark and sinful behavior and feelings.

Several things are happening in this brief account of Yaldabaoth's work of creation.

(1) Yaldabaoth wants to create humans after they've already been created—in a kind of duplicate creation both in the image of God (in which humans are already created) but also in the likeness of Yaldabaoth's ugly nature.

(2) The *reason* for Yaldabaoth's duplicate creation is unlike the reason for the original creation, which came forth because God loved His/Her own

idea. Now Yaldabaoth wants to create to *get* something he lacks from his creation. Yaldabaoth still needs light.

(3) The humans are now given psychical features that correspond to their original perfect figures designed by the Infinite Spirit. Because of these features, humans can be confused between their original perfect selfhood and the kind of selfhood that relates to the darkness and destructive nature of materialism. What's worse is that these psychical tendencies make humans feel as though their connections to the darkness are their own thoughts.

Now the work begins. The creating powers have authorized the creating angels to use the psychical substances to "create a network of limbs and trunk, with all the parts properly arranged" (Meyer, 119).

Each angel is in charge of creating one of the many parts of the body. How can an angel create a body part? Remembering that Humans are created by the gazing or *thinking* of the Creator/Mind, we can think of the whole body—and its parts—as the manifestation of the ideas. Angels or demons are best understood as spirits in contemporary thought, so we can envision this creative act as a spirit conceiving an idea that is made manifest in particular ways. In the case of Yaldabaoth's creating, we have learned that his creation is a mockery of the real and perfect creation. Also the material senses—caused by the counterfeit spirit—can report only a measurable and mortal sense of being. The creating act of Invisible Spirit is made manifest through distinct but immeasurable and immortal ideas.

Take a look at the text of the Secret Revelation itself (Appendix A) to see a list of all the human body parts and their unique creators. Starting with Raphaō, who created the head, each named angel creates the next human body part, from head to toe, until Phikna creates the toes of the left foot, and Miamai creates the toenails. To be certain that humans don't control their own bodies, Yaldabaoth's instructions continue:

> Those which are ordained in charge of the preceding [created body parts] are seven in number: Athōth, Armas, Kalila, Iabēl, Sabaōth, Cain, Abel. (Layton, 41)

But the limbs need to be activated, since they are not self-acting. So, again, new angels are appointed to the activation assignment for the parts that need to move:

> First the head, Diolimodraza; the back of the neck, Iammeax; the right shoulder, Iakouib; the left shoulder, Ouertōn, . . . the bodily

cavity, Arouph; the abdomen, Sabalō; the left foot, Marephnounth; its toes, Abrana. (Layton, 41–42)

As if that weren't enough supervision of bodily creation, seven more angels are called in with power over these angels. And then, another (Arkhendekta) is over the senses; another (Deitharbathas) is over the reception; another is over the imagination; . . . and the one over all impulse to action is Riaramnackhō. And we thought modern biology was complicated!

It's not over yet. Now the demons are called into action. The connection between these demons and the human body reads like a medical treatise. Every detail of the body, mind, and emotions is carefully dissected and analyzed.

> The wellspring of the demons that are in all the body is divided in four: heat, cold, wetness, dryness. And the mother of them all is matter. (Layton, 42)

What? The mother of the source of all the demons is matter? Yes, "for they are nourished by her" (Layton, 42). And then four *chief* demons arise from this source, and these four demons cause the *passions*. Now we have hit on the central nerve station. The passions have direct control over all those body parts governed by the creating demons.

PASSIONS AND DEMONS

In antiquity the general population feared the power of *passions* to cause emotional agitation. Remembering that the greatest state of divine perfection in the "Fullness" (*Pleroma*) is *stillness*, we can imagine how the most disruptive force to perfect health and harmony would be an agitation.

Jesus-followers agreed with the highly influential Stoic philosophers of the day that passions represented serious forms of evil agitations. But Stoics thought of passions as interior attitudes that should be controlled with discipline. If someone delivered the news that your child had just died, you should control your emotions and show no grief, because an unresisted passion could take over and control you.

The Jews and Jesus-followers also feared the power of the passions, but they envisioned passions within the domain of the demons, external to themselves. These unseen powers could cause people to lose control of themselves. No longer controlling their own emotions, the victims succumb. With such persuasive powers, demons can overtake someone's destiny and cause death or determine a good or evil fortune.[3] This is why Jesus's ability to cast out demons held such importance to his followers.

Despite the differences of opinion about the origin of passions between Stoics and Jesus communities, the Secret Revelation of John identifies four primary demons who are the same as Stoicism's four main categories of passions. These are distress (there is something evil at hand), fear (there will be something evil in the future), delight (there is something good in the present), and desire (there will be something good in the future that one does not yet have).[4] Bodily pains and emotional anguish are nearly indistinguishable in antiquity, because the ancients (unlike present-day people), viewed both body and psyche as subject to outside influences. A demon could cause "'anything which overtakes man," such as destiny or death or any good or evil fortune."[5]

Our contemporary usage of the term *spirit* works in a similar way to ancient usage of the word *demon*. These spirits behaved like messengers or agents of the gods. When the gods opposed other gods or guardian spirits, their messengers were empowered to cause passionate reaction in the people who leaned on them for support.

The story of the Secret Revelation of John is driven by a yearning for freedom from the devastating effects of passions. Michael A. Williams's vivid description of the work of demons drives home the urgency associated with the passions:

> The instability excited by the archons [rulers] and demons takes its characteristic form in the churning nausea of deep-seated passions (grief, fear, desire, anger, etc.)—as difficult to root out as ingested bacteria. These turbulent passions, aroused deep within the individual, had to be eradicated in order for one to be perfect and therefore *immovable* [able to inhabit the unshakable realm].[6]

So the drama in the Secret Revelation of John is mostly a huge, cosmic battle against the demons (spirits) over the control of human souls and bodies. Sophia (Wisdom) remains an important figure, because she first exemplified unbearable agitation over the realization of her mistake. When she "began to move around," the Lord explained to John that this moving around was because "she was agitated" (Meyer, 117). But because she is wise, she is able to deliver the demon-afflicted people from their suffering. She helps to organize the forces against the powers behind the passions. Ultimately, the warfare is not against the

---

3. Foerster, "Daimon," 2.

4. Dunderberg, *Beyond Gnosticism*, 109–10.

5. Foerster, "Daimon," 2.

6. Williams, *Immovable Race*, 152.

body or even the world, but against the fraudulent demons or powers who would imprison the soul within the chains of mortality.

The four leading demons stir up the agony that comes from grief, pleasure, desire, and fear. Think how far they extend:

> From grief come envy, fanaticism, pain, distress, contention for victory, lack of repentance, anxiety, mourning, and so forth.
>
> From pleasure come an abundance of evil, vain conceit, and the like.
>
> From desire come anger, wrath, bitterness, bitter lust, insatiableness, and the like.
>
> From fear come terror, entreaty, anguish, shame. (Layton, 43)

There are now three hundred sixty-five demons ("angels") who "all worked together until, limb by limb, the animate [psychical] and material body was completed" (Layton, 43). We have just unearthed another important clue to the peculiar nature of the human bodies. The psychical body has been created and governed by the same source as the troubling passions. The same demons who create bodies manipulate them through emotional anguish.

YALDABAOTH GETS ANGRY

But with all of Yaldabaoth's efforts to create everything for himself—in the image of what he had seen from the power he got from his mother—he failed. His demon-manufactured humans remained inanimate for a long period, with no life in them. Meanwhile, his mother (Sophia) grew concerned that his efforts to create were getting out of hand. When she

> wanted to retrieve the power which she had given to the Chief Ruler [Yaldabaoth], she entreated the Mother-Father of the All. (King, 18:3, 4)

In a clever move, the Mother-Father sends "luminaries," (those who give light) advising Yaldabaoth to

> breathe into his [the mortal's] face by your spirit and his body will arise. And into his face he [Yaldaboath] blew his spirit, which is the power of his Mother. He did not understand because he dwells in ignorance. (King, 18:7)

Now Yaldabaoth is caught! He has neither creative intelligence nor animating Spirit of his own. In his ignorance, he tried to copy the one and only true creation. But since his duplicate creation lacked life (or spirit), he was tempted with the luminaries' suggestions to use his mother's spirit.

> And the power of the Mother left Yaldabaoth and went into the psychic body that they [he and his minions] had made according to the likeness of the one who exists from the beginning. (King, 18:10)

The spirit, breath, or life from his mother has now left him! And with that move, the *psychical* human being has an indissoluble link to the divine origin, even though he can still be manipulated by the demons who created him. We can sense the drama about to unfold.

> The body moved and gained power, and it was luminous. And in that moment, the rest of the powers became jealous . . . His [Adam's, or the first Human's] understanding was stronger than those who had made him and greater even than the Chief Ruler. When they understood that he was luminous, could think better than they did, and was naked of evil, they picked him up and threw him down into the lowest part of all matter. (King, 18:11, 12, 16–18)

Yaldabaoth has been exposed as a fraud. He has no power or intelligence to actually create, and his arrogance causes him (and his minions) to become jealous of what they attempted to create. All Humans have the power of Life within, because the Spirit animates them. Although Life (Spirit) has always been present, the Chief Demon (Yaldabaoth) can think of nothing of his own and tries to seek glory by copying the original. Failing to create a *real* being, he boils over with jealousy and tries to destroy the thing greater than himself.

CLUES EXPOSE
THE FRAUDULENT COUNTERFEIT

The pieces come together. Yaldabaoth has no power and no intelligence, but his purpose is to take the glory of God for himself and to destroy the people who have the Spirit he craves. What led us to this conclusion?

Clue #1: Yaldabaoth's creating partner was "mindlessness."

Clue #2: Yaldabaoth competes with God.

Clue #3: Yaldabaoth's powers *look* real and powerful, making his creation appear valid.

Clue #4: Wisdom (his mother) discerns his arrogance and blasphemy.

Clue #5: Sophia's act of repentance is based on an honest recognition of the temptation of evil.

Clue #6: Yaldabaoth's creation looks and feels like the image of God.

Clue #7: As the counterfeit image of God, people see themselves as the likeness of Yaldabaoth and become monstrous as he is.

Clue #8: The feelings of *self* (the psychical self) are created by Yaldabaoth's manipulating demons.

Those who learn to detect counterfeit money inform us that the quickest way to detect fraud is to know the original thoroughly. The first gem from the Secret Revelation of John was its determination that we (its readers) would know the original creation thoroughly: we would know the strength and beauty of God's realm so well that the counterfeit would not confuse us. But as the Secret Revelation continues, we come to know that the counterfeit will struggle to tear down all that is good, until it finally destroys itself. In their fit of jealousy, Yaldabaoth and his powers recognized the enlightened Adam and threw him into the lowest part of the material realm of limitations. This is the same Adam they had just animated with power and light. (These are the events quoted and discussed above. See King, chapter 18.) And, since Adam, his son Seth, and Seth's children originally derived from the source of perfection, Adam becomes the archetype of all humanity in his battle with Yaldabaoth.

Throwing Adam down to the lowest part of the material realm of limitations is, of course, a nasty move, because only in this realm can the deceiver have any hope of overpowering the psychical type of being. We need to remember that the psychical person can toggle back and forth between the material (limited) and spiritual (limitless) sense of himself or herself.

> The archons [the powers controlled by Yaldabaoth] might be able to overpower the psychical perceptible body once again. (Meyer, 125)

Having been thrown into the material realm, people use only material senses to judge what is real, and demon-caused passions are then able to manipulate them.

WAR

However, the clues we noticed in Yaldabaoth's creating act are now weapons of self-defense against the vicious jealousy of the Chief Demon. One of the clues informed us that he was actually competing with the original creating God—the God who is all-powerful and all-good. People serve as his ransom, and his real enemy is the Mind who can create. But the Mother-Father knows the tactics of the enemy and is ready for the onslaught.

> So with its benevolent and most merciful Spirit, the Mother-Father sent a helper to Adam—enlightened Insight, who is from the Mother-Father and who was called Life. She helped the whole creature, laboring with it, restoring it to fullness. (Meyer, 125)

Equipped with Insight hidden within,

> Adam's ability to think was greater than that of all the creators. But when the archons [Yaldabaoth's rulers] looked up, they saw that Adam's ability to think was greater, and they devised a plan with the whole throng of archons and angels. (Meyer, 125)

From the spirit that comes from matter—ignorance, desire, and their own counterfeit spirit—the archons (rulers) plan to imprison their human archetype in the tomb of mortality. The chains holding him captive in the tomb are the power of forgetfulness. If he can't remember his true origin, he won't rebel or seek his way back to his true origin in the realm of God. The only weapon available to the human's enemies is deception, through the counterfeit spirit. But, wait! The Mother-Father had sent just the right equipment to retaliate. "Enlightened Insight within Adam, however, was rejuvenating Adam's mind" (Meyer, 125).

TWO CREATIONS OR ONE?

Here is where the text can cause some readers to think they are reading cross-eyed. Yes, we know that the One and Infinite Spirit/Mind caused and created the realm of beings who are loved and cared for by the Mother-Father.

But Yaldabaoth's creation sounds increasingly like the one we're more familiar with. As humans, we *do* exhibit moments of great spiritual clarity, and at the same time we can be tempted with the worst of human passions, and we certainly die. We have the capacity for both good and evil, and this is the nature of the *psychic* human as the ancient writers identified humanity.

These two contrary stories of creation give the impression that creation has happened twice and by two separate deities. But those clues we picked up along the way help us recognize we are required to actually enter the zone of the first realm to understand what is happening with the second. Think it, live it, believe it, act like it, trust it.

From the first clue, if we remember that the creation by Yaldabaoth occurred with the partner of *mindlessness*, we'll realize that this creation has no intelligence of its own. Therefore we cannot rely on the intelligence that appears to come from this source. From another clue, we must remember that the feelings associated with Yaldabaoth's creation are counterfeit. If we identify with this creation, we take on the image and likeness of *that* creator, and we feel like monsters also.

To keep our mental bearings in the midst of the warfare, we need to actively remind ourselves that whenever we encounter the stirring of passions, we are being manipulated by a counterfeit spirit. Those feelings stemming from grief, pleasure, desire, and fear do not originate in the omnipotent and good God, but from the jealous god.

The weapon used against us by Yaldabaoth's rulers is hoodwinking us into *forgetting* the continuity of goodness and to believe our feelings instead. But this is a mental trick, and our Mother-Father has sent us enlightened Insight, which is rejuvenating our minds. We are able to resist the mental pull toward self and trust the power of goodness, because it is the only true existence.

As is true in any battle, the harder the enemy pushes, the more vigorous the reply until one side gives up. In this case, the cosmic warfare between the goodness of God and the destructive forces of the Chief Demon calls forth the wisdom, depth, and strength of the One who loves. As we yield to this one source of true power, we will become increasingly convinced of the fraudulence and impotence of the counterfeit spirit.

But the author of this text is speaking to us as if we have been willing to take up arms and engage in the battle ourselves. We will not be able to follow the logic and power of the message without consenting to awaken from our mortal dreams. Then we will realize the oneness of creation.

Now that we know that Adam has been thrown down "into the lowest part of the material realm" (Meyer, 125), we also know that Adam's defense will rely on his spiritual side. As a psyche, he may feel manipulated by the dreamy evidence of material mortality, but he is also capable of being awakened and remembering the truth about God's realm and his right to dwell there. "The Epinoia of the light who was in him is the one who will awaken his thinking" (King, 19:15).

Naturally, the Rulers, ambassadors from the Chief Demon, seek the means to retaliate. They take Adam and place him in paradise, telling him to go ahead and eat. We recognize the irony of sending Adam to paradise as the setting for the cosmic battle to take place. Adam is expected to enjoy himself with all the delights of the garden, but danger lurks behind its attractiveness. Again, the Rulers attempt to deceive him.

> For indeed their delight is bitter and their beauty is licentious. For their delight is deception and their trees are impiety. And their fruit is an incurable poison and their promise is death. (King, 20:3–5)

ANOTHER LOOK AT PARADISE

From here, the familiar Genesis account of Adam's experience in paradise dissolves into a different plot. The characters remain the same: Adam, the creator of Adam, the snake, and Eve. But instead of portraying Eve or Adam as the ignorant cause of evil for the world, the author of the Secret Revelation of John exposes the true enemy as the counterfeit spirit—the so-called creator god, who is ignorant and jealous. And Adam and Eve become the means of *salvation* for humanity!

Here is a new setting for Genesis. Take two: Adam is walking in the garden, when Epinoia (the Insight that awakens his thinking) warns Adam.

> Its root is bitter and its branches are deaths. Its shade is hate and deception dwells in its leaves. And its blossom is the anointment of evil. And its fruit is death, and desire is its seed. And it blossoms from the darkness. (King, 20:10–15)

Now protected from such deceit, Adam is instructed by Epinoia to eat from *the tree of the knowledge of what is good and evil*! It will help him distinguish the fruit of death from the fruit of life. But the rulers, aware now of Adam's desire to find this valuable tree, try to block his view of it. They know its fruit might help him recognize the shamefulness of his nakedness brought on by Yaldabaoth's creation. He might even "look up to his fullness" (King, 20:20) where he'd remember his origin in the calm perfection of goodness.

Like those of us reading the text, the character John (from the first chapter of the book) knows this isn't the way the story is told in Genesis. He interrupts the Savior (the character who is the storyteller), to ask, "Sir, was it not the snake that taught Adam to eat?" Right, the Savior replies. But the snake instructed Adam to eat all the seductive fruits of death "so that he (Adam) might become useful to it (the snake)" (Layton, 45).

Failing in his attempt to guard Adam from the tree of the knowledge of good and evil, Yaldabaoth's first Ruler boiled over with the realization that the enlightened Insight within Adam made Adam stronger of mind than Yaldabaoth was. Now Yaldabaoth's next blow must be an attack on Adam's mind. He will put Adam to sleep in a trance. It's not like the sleep that Moses described in the book of Genesis,[7] during which Adam's rib is removed. Rather it is a dulling of the mind.

> I shall make their minds sluggish, that they may neither under-
> stand nor discern. (Meyer, 126)

Yaldabaoth wants to create a female while Adam is in this dazed state. But enlightened Insight tenaciously remains in Adam despite the trance that overtakes him. When Yaldabaoth attempts to "take her [Insight] from Adam's side" (Meyer, 126), enlightened as she is, she won't let it happen. So Yaldabaoth creates another figure in the form of a female. But she is incomplete, and now he takes a part of Adam's power to put into the female. This woman, designed by Yaldabaoth but empowered by Adam's power, comes to stand next to Adam. And suddenly the enlightened Insight arises from within Adam and removes the veil covering Adam's mind.

The counterfeit spirit (Yaldabaoth) has failed again! He creates Adam, but Adam is smarter than he is. He creates Eve, and Eve awakens Adam to his own completeness. They back off, leaving Yaldabaoth alone. But of course, their departure enrages Yaldabaoth again, so he curses the earth. The author of the Secret Revelation of John agrees with the third chapter of Genesis, that the god who formed Adam and Eve does curse the ground (Genesis 3:17). But for the Secret Revelation of John, Yaldabaoth and his

---

7. Today, most scholars agree the book of Genesis was not written by Moses, but second-century Jewish scholars generally believed in Moses's authorship of Genesis.

jealousy are to blame for the curse, rather than the sinful behavior of the human being.

Anger now drives Yaldabaoth in a blind and ignorant pursuit of Eve. When he finds her preparing herself for her husband, she and Adam become too frightened to denounce him. He hurls them out of paradise and envelops them in thick darkness. But Yaldabaoth can't let go of them, and once again he finds her by Adam's side. This time he prepares to rape her.

THE RAPE OF EVE

But with all that is good and omnipotent on the side of the true God, help is on the way. From God's divine, unshakable realm, one of the aeons (characters), named Forethought already knows the danger posed by ignorant anger.

> So when the Forethought of the All realized this [the impending rape], she dispatched emissaries, and they stole Life out of Eve. (Meyer, 127)

Eve is protected during the ordeal, because her Life is safely removed from the raped body.[8] But the ignorant first ruler doesn't know any better. Through his violation of Eve's innocence, the Chief Demon causes two offspring to be born from Eve, and they will be as much a counterfeit as their father.

> He [Yaldabaoth] called them by the names Cain and Abel, with a view to deceive . . . Through intercourse the first ruler produced duplicate bodies and he blew some of his false spirit into them. (Meyer, 128)

Yaldabaoth succeeded in causing birth in the likeness of bodies, but he enlivened them with his false (counterfeit) spirit. The people he tried to create would never be the true image and likeness of the divine, since they were raised up by a counterfeit spirit.

In describing Yaldabaoth's violent act, the Secret Revelation of John lets slip another clue as to the full nature of the beast. Yaldabaoth goes by different names throughout the book, but in this passage, he is identified as "first ruler." It is not too difficult, especially for second-century Jews of Alexandria, to recognize that this "ruler" probably refers to the ruling

---

8. This reflects what happens when women disassociate from their bodies during traumatic violence. See Lillie, *Rape of Eve.*

Roman emperor as well as the Chief Demon. Open critiques of Rome were impossible in the second century, because they were likely punishable by torture or death. So the author's clandestine account functions as one of the "hidden transcripts," or conventions understood by the community of the oppressed, offering messages of encouragement and hope.[9] Part of the *secret* in the Secret Revelation of John may be the disguised description of the demonic nature of the Roman Empire.

Meanwhile, Adam, who had been awakened by the enlightened Insight, discerns what is going on between Yaldabaoth and Eve. Unlike Yaldabaoth's impulse to act out his own lust, violence, and deception, Adam can perceive the likeness of his own Foreknowledge in Eve! Merely with the recognition of his own spiritual essence and likeness in Eve, Adam reenacts the productivity of the Father with his self-reflective gaze, and produces

> a son like the child of humanity. He called him Seth, after the manner of the generation in the eternal realms. (Meyer, 128)

TIMELESS GENERATION

Seth has not been created a second time. The account of Seth's birth tightens the relationship between Yaldabaoth's mythical creation and the original fullness and perfection of the divine realm, because he is a major figure in both.

Those of us who live with clocks, calendars, and time-organized lives must be reminded that the original creation carries on without the limitations of time and space. We cannot follow the meaning of Yaldabaoth and his mythical creation without keeping it in the context of the reality established in the beginning of the book. The fullness of God's creative work, the infinitude of goodness and omnipotence, is ever ongoing.

Therefore, the stories of two creations make no sense if we try to place them in a kind of chronological order. Placing the story of Yaldabaoth after the story of the divine completeness and fullness does not indicate a later period of time. Rather, this mythical creation is a concept that explains the nature of evil, but it is not a second or separate act of creation. A counterfeit tells its own story, but never morphs into reality.

The birth of Seth helps to clarify the relationship between the two accounts of creation, because he appears in both. As a character in traditional Christian

9. For further explanation of the "hidden transcripts," see Elliott, *Roman Family Empires*, 29–33.

teachings, Seth is not well-known. But the authority for his role does originate in Genesis 4 and 5, where he is named as the third son born to Adam.

> When Adam had lived one hundred thirty years, he became the father of a son in his likeness, according to his image, and named him Seth. (Genesis 5:3 NRSV)

This is meant to be the same Seth who in the Secret Revelation of John, is the image of the perfect Father, because all the aeons came forth by the Mind that wished to create. "Its will became a reality and appeared" (Meyer, 112). Here, Seth is appointed

> to the second eternal realm, before the second luminary, Oroiael. In the third eternal realm were stationed the offspring of Seth, with the third luminary, Daveithai. The souls of the saints were stationed there. (Meyer, 114)

In the Yaldabaoth account of creation, Adam succeeded in imitating the divine order, where Yaldabaoth had failed, and Seth is indeed "a son like the child of humanity." He is called "Seth, after the manner of the generation in the eternal realms" (Meyer, 128).

Thus, both accounts agree with Genesis, but they explain the same story of the generation of Seth and his seed (children) from the perspective of contrasting worldviews.

What a difference from the Chief Ruler's type of procreation through lust! Yaldabaoth had tried to plant sexual desire in humanity in order to multiply counterfeit copies. His endgame was to find the means for keeping control over mortal bodies. But contrary to the acts of the first ruler (still Yaldabaoth), Adam and Eve both recognize the spiritual essence of each other. No violence could undo the spiritual Forethought still within Eve, and their progeny would become savior figures for all time.[10]

The contrast between the unshakable realm and the violent one could not be greater. And now that similarity between the demons-ruling-the-body and the demons-ruling-the-empire has been established, the image of rape is poignantly relevant. Rome has raped its victims, overpowering them with violence.[11] But, according to the Secret Revelation of John, the

10. I follow King's interpretation of this passage as a "remarkable image of appropriately spiritual sexuality—the recognition of the image of God in the other as a shared essence" (King, *The Secret Revelation of John*, 129).

11. For a full elaboration on the connection between the rape of God's beloved

Savior has promised there is a "Forethought of the All," who knows the pain and struggle. She guards the heart and soul even if the body is tortured and raped. The good news—hidden from the ignorant Chief Demon—is that the offspring of Adam and Eve is prepared to save the world from the evil of the demons (the demons of Rome or of the cosmos). This is the second gem of the Secret Revelation of John: that the violence of the world is truly fraudulent. It leaves enough clues to assure us of its counterfeit nature, and we are not deceived.

With these two gems firmly in hand now, we readers are prepared for the book's third gem: the understanding of healing and salvation as one. Violence of the patriarchal system culminates in rape and is replaced by the true method of creation. Sophia's spiritual power has remained in Adam, maintaining his spiritual perfection, and this is the divine essence he perceives in Eve. Mere recognition of the divine essence in each other is spiritually life-producing, demonstrating for humanity how successful sexual reproduction is modeled on the divine pattern. Eve, then, becomes the model of salvation, which will be amplified in the third and final section of the book.

Readers of the Secret Revelation of John, from the second century through today, breathe a profound sigh of relief with the news that there is an escape route from victimization. Since universal creation is life-producing, our knowledge of it frees us to discover our own worth and safety. Ignorance of this universal creation results in the experience of random violence. Centuries later, the Age of Enlightenment pursued the kind of reasoning that would empower individuals to improve their own condition. How will twenty-first-century thinkers make use of this path to the continuity of good?

---

daughters and the metaphorically raped Egyptians, see Lillie, *Rape of Eve*, 269.

4

The Third Gem
Healing and Salvation Are One

This third gem, like the other two, needs a great deal of scraping and polishing to discern its beauty. Centuries' worth of new interpretations, changes in language, and doctrinal shifts have obscured the meaning of *salvation*—or "being saved"—from the intent of the second-century author. Everyone was looking for salvation then, but I don't think we could say everyone is looking for salvation today. At least, I don't have many friends who would say that's what they're looking for.

Many people today define *salvation* as the deliverance from the punishment of sin at some point after death. But fear of God's judgment no longer holds the threat it used to carry. Either people don't think they've sinned very much, or else they're not convinced death will bring on the curse of eternal damnation. And yet if someone could promise an escape route from fear, disease, chaos, emotional torment, and physical danger, many of us would come running. This is what *salvation* meant in antiquity, and this is the promise of the Secret Revelation of John.

Saving our bodies from pain or disease in the twenty-first-century world, however, usually requires different types of doctors from those who save our souls. Bodily healing today has largely lost its spiritual hue and has gradually succumbed to the soulless laws of physics. By contrast, when salvation was brought about by a God-sent Savior in antiquity, freedom from disease or pain was more than a medical event; it was a direct and meaningful encounter with the divine power.

As we saw in Chapter 3, above, demons were known to stir up passions, and the disturbed emotions and feelings would result in bodily suffering. In this ancient schema, the soul (*psyche*) is where all the action is.

SOUL AND BUTTERFLY

No one has ever seen a soul entering or exiting someone's body. We use the word readily, as if we know what it means, but do we? Where is it? What is it? How do we know?

People have asked these questions as far back as we can remember. But for the most part, they have agreed with Homer that souls reside in their bodies until death. Then, when they die, their soul somehow evacuates the body.

The closest word in English to the ancient Greek word *psyche*, is "soul." Plato considered the *psyche* to be the essence of a person, regardless of their state of life or death. For Aristotle, the soul (*psyche*) was not a distinctive substance, so it could not be separated from the body. Naturally, then, people were left wondering what happens when someone dies: Does the soul depart the inert body and maintain the essence of the person, or does the soul die when the body dies?

In the Hellenistic philosophical schools of Greece and Rome, philosophers presumed that if they could figure out the connection between body and thoughts, their help with the mental troubles would also contribute to healing the body. Modern neuroscientists are still seeking an understanding of the relationship between mind and brain.

The answers haven't come easily. Questions persist: What *is* this soul that animates the living organism? When humans run into questions that remain unanswered by empirical knowledge or some kind of scientific explanation, they resort to myths to explain the meaning. The quest for the meaning of "soul" (*psyche*) fits that category well.

Eros and Psyche

One of the enduring myths about the soul originated in the second century and features *Eros and Psyche*.[1] (Eros in Greek is known as Cupid in Latin.) Psyche was

---

1. The myth of Eros and Psyche is from the Ovidian *Metamorphoses*, attributed to Lucius Apuleius Madaurensis or Platonicus, of the second century. See Antonakou and Triarhou, "Soul, Butterfly, Mythological Nymph."

the most beautiful daughter of a certain king and queen, but her admirers doted on her too much. They neglected their proper worship for Eros's mother, the goddess Venus, and she grew jealous of all the attention bestowed on Psyche. So she sent her son Eros, the powerful master of love, to enact her revenge on the beautiful Psyche.

Eros was supposed to shoot Psyche with his arrow so that she would fall in love with something hideous. But in doing so, he inadvertently scratched himself with his own arrow and fell deeply in love with her. She was guided in the darkness to this one who loved her, but who would disappear before the morning light. In her attempt to see and identify who it was who loved her so passionately, she also wounded herself with one of Eros's arrows. Struck with feverish passion, she inadvertently woke him up, and he instantly fled. Although she tried to pursue him, he abandoned her on the riverbank. There she suffered the terrible grief that could only be banished by Eros.

Knowing of her suffering, Eros seeks help from Zeus, the father of the gods, who takes pity on Psyche and grants her immortality. Psyche (Soul) had been a mere mortal but is granted immortality. Freed from death, the body of this soul can fly freely, soaring above mortal sorrows.

This is how the image of a beautiful butterfly became the imaginative artistic rendition of Psyche. The metamorphosis of the butterfly—from caterpillar to chrysalis to butterfly—inspired artists and writers to depict the soul's exit from the body. The butterfly represents the freedom of the soul. In fact, the word for "butterfly" in formal Greek is *psyche*. Psyche is thought to be the soul of any who have died, free to abandon the limitations of the body.

We recall that the psyche is that aspect of human life that can yield either to divine or devilish powers. When evil spirits (demons) are too strong, the psyche (soul) either follows all the wrong impulses and suffers the consequences, or else it discerns the presence and power of the divine, follows the light, and stays safe.

Before Descartes and subsequent philosophers made the split between the mind world and the matter world, the notion of the government of the body by thoughts was not as alien as it is today. Even the distinction between the periods before and after death were not as pronounced as they appear to be now, when the body, not the soul, holds the conditions of life. But in antiquity, the distance between life and death was not as great, because suffering reflected the state of the soul more than the state of the body.

The same John in the opening scene of the Secret Revelation of John, now, in the final portion of the book, appears again and asks the Savior some penetrating questions about the psyche (soul). This *self* that is in the middle, between spiritual and material influences, is what feels like *me*! Here is the evidence that the Secret Revelation of John is not a mere theological treatise. It's a message about transformation. It grabs our soul—where we think we are—and intends to transform us, as the butterfly.

In the Secret Revelation of John, the first gem we uncovered was all about the impenetrable continuity of good. Infinite Spirit is the abundant source of life and goodness. All the children of God are blessed and live fearlessly in the unshakable realm. The second gem we found was the realization that the evil spirit is nothing but a fraud or counterfeit. Its supposed force tries to pull us into darkness and limitation by tricking us and making us forget our roots in the unshakable realm. Its motives and methods are exposed by the Savior.

If we modern readers want to be able to understand what John hears from the Savior, we will first have to put aside not only our education in Newtonian physics, but also what many Christians of the Western Church have been taught about salvation for the past millennium or so. Church doctrines, especially those related to salvation, have evolved dramatically. For example, the modern idea that salvation rescues us only from sin, or that we might feel the effects of salvation only after death, would have provided very little comfort for John's immediate concerns. The state of his psyche (soul) was just as important to him right then as it would be when he no longer lived in the flesh.

John's questions spring from a heart yearning to find the way to freedom from things that hurt—before or after death. Whether the demons cause a hurting body, oppression from political forces, pain from evil influences, or even death itself, John is looking for answers.

Today we feel vulnerable too. Evil presents itself in many forms, and we are all looking for the pathway to the place of permanent security—or the unshakable realm. As we will discover in the last chapter of this book, when all three gems are rediscovered, polished, and appreciated, they will be of great value in our contemporary world as they were so long ago. Their power and beauty will be able to transform us as readily now as it did in antiquity.

We discover this gem right at the place where we feel caught in the middle between the heavenly realm and the prison of darkness. Our psyche now takes center stage. Are we doomed to live under the deceiving powers of the counterfeit spirit, or will the Savior bring us safely home forever?

Speaking for all of us who discern the forces of darkness as well as the source of light, John seizes the opportunity to ask the Savior directly about salvation: Who gets saved? How? When? What does it mean?

QUESTION #1

Lord, will all the souls be led safely into pure light? (Meyer, 128)

Being led safely is John's key question. Considering the demon-caused dangers of everyday life in antiquity, a Savior who would protect people from the demons' enslaving passions would certainly be good news. John knows the protection and wisdom of the "pure light" is the goal of salvation, because it brings freedom from the widespread ignorance about God's goodness. It never occurs to John that salvation would constitute rewards for good behavior, when the real need for salvation is the power to combat the nasty work of the demons. In response to John's first question, the Savior is explaining that salvation was the rescue from the powers that make us forget the true origin of our being or from the demon-induced passions that agitate and harm us.

Without help from the Savior, these evil, angry, and fearful thoughts make us lose control and feel like victims of sickness, political oppression, violence, and death itself. The Savior respects John's intuition behind the question, and he answers John:

> These are great things that have arisen in your thinking. For it is
> difficult to disclose these things to any others except those who are
> from the immovable generation.[2] (King, 23:3)

That must have been encouraging to John, because the Savior implies that John is ready to hear what the Savior is about to disclose. Jesus's[3] answer to

2. This is a reminder that the term "immovable generation" is translated interchangeably with "immovable race" and "unshakable generation" by the translators we consult for this book.

3. The Coptic version of this passage usually refers to the Savior or Jesus as "Lord." I have taken the liberty to interject both "Savior" and "Jesus," because all three terms are used synonymously in the Secret Revelation of John. Some scholars argue that the opening and closing portions of the book were added on later in order to "Christianize" the text, because Jesus's name is only mentioned there. But I am treating the Secret

his question about *who* will be saved brings with it a vivid image of what salvation will be like when they receive it.

> Those upon whom the Spirit of Life will descend and with whom it will be powerfully present, they will be saved and will become perfect. And they will become worthy of the great realms. And they will be purified in that place from all evil and the concerns of wickedness. Then they will not take care for anything except the imperishability alone, attending to it from this point on without anger or envy or jealousy or desire or greed of anything at all. (King, 23:4–8)

The Savior assures John that people who are truly saved will become perfect and cleansed of all evil and fear of being bad. Demons will no longer be able to provoke any passions, since those who are saved will achieve freedom from their supposed powers to incite anger, jealousy, envy, desire, or greed of anything.

This extraordinary liberation is extended to "those upon whom the Spirit of Life will descend and with whom it will be powerfully present." But what about those who still feel angry, jealous, and greedy? Will they make it?

QUESTION #2

> Lord, will the souls of those upon whom the power of the Spirit of Life descended but who did not do these works be excluded? (King, 23:13)

It may be one thing to admit that great things will happen to people who have mastered these passions. But will the transforming Spirit find its way even to those who aren't behaving as they should? Jesus has complete confidence in the power of the transforming and saving Spirit. He replies to John:

> If the Spirit descends upon them, they will be saved in any case, and they will migrate.[4] For *power will descend upon every human*

Revelation of John as it is presented in one whole text, which affirms Jesus's identification as Savior.

4. Meyer translates this phrase, "they will be saved and *transformed*" (129; italics added).

being—for without it, no one is able to stand upright. (King, 23:14, 15; italics added)

Power from the Spirit of Life will descend on *everyone*! That is truly a mind-boggling concept. Everyone?

Being saved and transformed has nothing to do with someone's personality or social standing or health. The power descends on everyone, because Spirit is infinite—big enough to be there for everyone. That is, it is the business of Spirit to "descend upon every human being," and Spirit has the power to make everyone perfect and worthy of greatness. It cleanses all evil and wickedness. In fact, as the Savior points out, nobody can even stand on his or her own two feet without this power from above. The burden rests on the Spirit to do its saving and transcending work for everyone.

After they are born, then if the Spirit of Life increases and the power comes to strengthen that soul, it is not possible to lead it astray into the works of wickedness. (King, 23:16, 17)

But!—and this is an important caveat—in answer to John's question about those who aren't cleansed from all the evil, Jesus does admit that "those upon whom the counterfeit spirit descends are drawn by it and they are led astray" (King, 23:18). The beguiling counterfeit spirit is to blame for those who are misled. So, the Savior does not say that they forfeit their access to help, but they should be on guard that they could still be led astray.

We will return shortly to this question about how everyone could experience this transforming power of the Spirit, even if they are led astray. But first John is concerned with another matter.

QUESTION #3

Lord, then when the souls of those leave their flesh, where will they go? (King, 23:19)

If the Spirit gives us what we need to be pure, and we do follow the Spirit of Christ in our daily lives, what happens to our soul, then, when we leave the flesh? Where do we go? What happens next? The Lord laughs at the question. Maybe he thinks it is so obvious that the Spirit will naturally overpower all the last vestiges of the evil spirit.

He laughed and said to me [John], The soul in which the power will become stronger than the despicable spirit—for this one (the

soul) is powerful and it flees from evil—it will be saved by the visi-
tation of the Incorruptible and it will be admitted into the repose
of the aeons. (King, 23:20–23)

John may not be laughing yet, but he seems to have been aware that
the battle against evil does not end at the point of death. Exiting the flesh
is not the solution to the problems of the soul. The Savior confirms that
the "despicable spirit" is still strong, even when the body ceases to serve as
a holding place for the soul. But the good news is that it will never be as
strong as the power flowing from the Incorruptible One.

Here, then, is the key to understanding salvation in the second century. When a Savior saves souls, not matter, then death is not perceived as a
deciding factor in the success of the saving act. The body is merely the play-
ing field where we witness the battle between the forces of evil and good.

What is the bottom line, then, for the soul after it leaves the body? The
Incorruptible One intervenes, and because it is greater than the counterfeit,
it saves the struggling soul and leads it to eternal rest. So, now let's go back
to the people who succumb to the false attractions of the counterfeit spirit.

QUESTION #4

I [John] said, "Lord, then where will the souls be who do not know
to whom their souls belong"? (King, 23:25)

We were already warned in the Savior's first answer that the evil spirit could
seduce people, and they could be led astray, not realizing where they really
belong. John is concerned about how they will manage after leaving the
body. Will there be any means of rescue for them?

Jesus agrees that for these people, the contemptible counterfeit spirit
has grown stronger, and this spirit "burdens the soul and draws it into
works of wickedness, and he casts it down into forgetfulness" (King, 23:27).
He continues:

After it [the soul] comes forth [leaves the body], they hand it over
to the authorities who came into being through the Ruler. And
they [the Ruler's helpers] bind it [the soul] in chains and cast it
into prison. And they consort with it [the soul] until it awakens
from forgetfulness and receives knowledge. And in this way, it is
perfected and saved. (King, 23:27–30)

There is a lot more going on after death than we would know only by observing the body! Death is not the moment of judgment at all. According to the Savior, those who had succumbed to the false attractions of the counterfeit spirit will indeed suffer from their delusion after passing away from their bodies. They will feel imprisoned even without bars surrounding the body. But even then they can awaken from the dream of the false influence. The means of atoning for their mistakes before a Superjudge is of little concern because, most of all, they need to know how the Savior will protect them from the influence of the evil spirits that damned human experience.

This is the moment of great discovery! Escape from the evil influence comes not with death, but with awakening from the mental dullness or forgetfulness of original perfection. But then, that raises another question! How do we actually get back to that original perfection? John keeps asking.

QUESTION #5

> Lord, how does the soul become smaller and return back into the
> nature of its mother or the human? (King, 23:32)

Sometimes, when the words we read seem quite peculiar (such as the wording of this question), it helps to consider the way other translators read these texts from the Coptic. Here are two other ways to think of it: "How can the soul shrink down so as to be able to enter its mother or a man?" (Davies, 143). And, "How can the soul become younger and return into its mother's womb, or into the human?" (Meyer, 129).

The image of reentering a mother's womb is reminiscent of another story, from the Gospel of John, where Nicodemus, a highly respected Pharisee, asked Jesus a similar question: "How can anyone be born after having grown old? Can one enter a second time into the mother's womb and be born?" (John 3:4). In the Secret Revelation of John, the Lord's response to John encourages him to keep thinking about these things.

> Then he rejoiced when I asked this, and he said to me, "Truly you
> are blessed, for you have understood! That soul is made to follow
> another who has the Spirit of Life in it. It is saved by that (other)
> one. Then it is not cast into another flesh." (King, 23:33–36)

Instead of *shrinking* back into mortal origins, John learns that by following the Spirit of Life, no one will be thrown into any flesh. There will be no more fleshly limitations, neither in the form of reincarnation, nor of one's former birth experience. Instead, the Savior is pointing the way forward, where we discover the Spirit of Life, and we're saved from the passions that speak to us through the flesh.

These answers from the Lord provide relief for John; he realizes how everyone has a chance to be saved from the deceptive powers of the demons that cause suffering in all mortal flesh. Jesus assures us that the power of the Spirit will descend on all of us, before and after the experience of death, and it will transform us. But there is still one more possibility that concerns John.

QUESTION #6

Lord, what about those who understood and yet turned away? Where will their souls go? (King, 23:37)

If everyone is ultimately able to come to repose with the unshakable generation, what happens to those foolish people who have been given all they need, and have gained the true *gnosis* (knowledge of being awake), but they consciously *reject* it? As could be expected, it's not a good choice! The Savior replies:

> They will be admitted into that place where the angels of poverty go, the place where repentance does not occur. And they will guard them until that day when those who have blasphemed against the Spirit will be tortured. And they will be punished with an eternal punishment. (King, 23:38–40)

This is certainly devastating news for people who intentionally disobey. They bring eternal punishment on themselves. But the most shocking part of this news is that there is no judge awaiting the soul's departure from earth. This is a *decision* made by people who already had what they needed to know before they acted on a wrong impulse! They may have thought they didn't want to obey, but the Savior makes clear that such a decision will be painful.

John had already heard in Jesus's reply to his second question that "*power will descend upon every human being*—for without it, no one is able to stand upright" (King, 23:14,15; italics added). Since there is no judge who determines whether someone will be sent to heaven or hell, the onus is on every individual to decide whether he or she will turn away or remain faithful to the knowledge of good they have been given.

Some scholars argue that, according to the author of the Secret Revelation of John, salvation is *not* available to everyone,[5] since the Savior says that the day will come when "they will be punished with an eternal punishment" (King, 23:38–40). But a closer look shows that everyone has been given what they need to be able to choose correctly, and that since the decision belongs to the individual and not an outsider, that individual is always able to make the change and follow the light of the Spirit. The savior is offering fair warning that if anyone makes this bad decision, there will never be an escape until he or she changes course. Suffering will indeed last forever because it is the mistaken decision itself that causes the misery. Therefore, misery endures until the change in thought takes place.

BONUS QUESTION

Convinced now that all souls will indeed be led safely into pure light (John's first question), one more issue concerns him.

> Lord, where did the despicable spirit come from? (King, 24:1)

The shorter version of the Secret Revelation of John sometimes offers a helpful comparison.[6] For this verse the short version reads, "Christ, where did the *counterfeit* spirit come from?" (King, 24:1; italics added). Both "despicable" and "counterfeit" describe this false spirit well, as we learned with the second gem. John would recognize the despicable nature of the evil spirit as a counterfeit, because the first gem assured us of the completeness and fullness of goodness. The first gem holds the answer to this last question about the source of this counterfeit spirit:

> He said to me, "The Mother-Father is great in mercy, the holy Spirit, who in every way is compassionate, who sympathizes with you, the Insight of enlightened Forethought. This one raised up the offspring of the perfect generation and their thought and the eternal light of the human." (Meyer, 129)

That is, the Savior reminded John that the one truth, the one reality, is the Mother-Father who loves you. Even when you were deluded by the counterfeit spirit, the holy Spirit, who sympathizes with your struggles, raises

---

5. A good example is Ramelli's argument against universal salvation in the Secret Revelation of John in Ramelli, "Apokatastasis," 33–35.

6. The two versions—longer and shorter—are described in Chapter 2.

you up into the eternal light where you can see clearly. The despicable spirit is simply a fraud, and its evil powers are impotent. Therefore, it came from nowhere. But in almost every religious work, right when the crowning point of the victory of good is about to appear, this is when the forces of evil violently catapult all their final ammunition. In the Secret Revelation of John, Yaldabaoth has finally

> realized that these people [the humans, images of God that he tried to duplicate] were exalted above him and could think better than he. (Meyer, 130)

Nothing could outrage him more! He is prepared to fight to the death.

YALDABAOTH'S GRAND FINALE

Yaldabaoth's full fury is unleashed. All his efforts to control humanity have failed; he has been exposed as a fraud. He now musters up all his powers to execute three final attempts to cause the ultimate destruction. To make sense of this spectacle, we readers need to remember that all his so-called powers are empty. In fact, he can accomplish nothing, but we will read the account from his point of view to understand what is happening. When the human psyche *feels* the pull toward Yaldabaoth's evil influences, we will recognize the source and remember its fraudulence simultaneously.

The First Attempt: The Flood

In his first attempt, the Chief Demon grabs the greatest source of power known to him—Sophia. In ancient societies, committing adultery blurred the lines between families and undermined the entire creation, so Yaldabaoth and his fellow authorities plan to commit adultery with Sophia. From this disruption of the order of the cosmos, they can beget bitter Fate for humans.

> Fate is like this because the powers are fickle. To the present day fate is tougher and stronger than what gods, angels, demons, and all the generations have encountered. For from fate have come all iniquity and injustice and blasphemy, the bondage of forgetfulness, and ignorance, and all burdensome orders, weighty sins, and great fears. (Meyer, 130)

Again, through his counterfeit actions, Yaldabaoth claims to have control over fate so that even the gods and demons would have to succumb to its power.

But whether he doubts the power of fate himself, or he wants to make sure there are no loopholes, Yaldabaoth decides to destroy the whole human creation once and for all with a flood. Here, the author of the Secret Revelation of John brings us back to the book of Genesis, demonstrating the meaning of Noah's flood in relation to the work of the counterfeit god.

In the retelling of the story in the Secret Revelation of John,

> The enlightened majesty of Forethought . . . warned Noah. Noah announced this to all the offspring, the human children, but those who were strangers to him did not listen to him. It did not happen the way Moses said, "They hid in an ark." Rather, they hid in a particular place, not only Noah, but also many other people from the unshakable generation. They entered that place and hid in a bright cloud. Noah knew about his supremacy. With him was the enlightened one who had enlightened them, since the first ruler had brought darkness upon the whole earth. (Meyer, 130)

GENESIS AND THE SECRET REVELATION OF JOHN

As we saw earlier, the author of the Secret Revelation of John turns back to Genesis frequently, probably to add weight to the authority of his teaching. Writers of the first and second centuries relied heavily on the stability and honor of tradition, so competition between ideas often showed up in different interpretations of the traditional elders.

Just as Jesus made use of the Hebrew Torah in his teaching,[7] so the author of the Secret Revelation of John uses Genesis as a point of authority and then gives it a bit of a twist. Both teachers explain that ancient Hebrew ideas need a modernized interpretation. In Matthew's Gospel, Jesus climbs up to a hilltop to proclaim what has since been identified as the Sermon on the Mount. Here he elaborates on his ancestors' instructions: "You have heard that it was said to those of ancient times, 'You shall not . . . murder . . . commit adultery . . . swear falsely,'" and so forth. "But *I* say to you" . . . even more than this is expected of you in my Father's realm (my paraphrase, Matthew 5:21–44).

Not too surprisingly, teachers from the first and second centuries were still interested in Genesis, but they also participated in the pop culture of the

7. At least according to the account in the Gospel of Matthew, discussed here.

day—*Neoplatonism*. Plato's fourth-century-BCE book *Timaeus* was the talk of the Mediterranean world. What's the meaning of matter? What's the cause of evil?

Philo, the first-century Jewish philosopher from Alexandria, is one of those philosophers who made a natural connection between these Platonic-oriented philosophical questions and his religious text, Genesis. Plato's "division of Being" inspired a new reading of Genesis for him, as if it were presenting two separate accounts of creation. First is the creation of the immaterial world of Ideas, and then a second record of creation tells it differently, with Adam and Eve representing the material world.

Maybe only a few decades later the author of the Secret Revelation of John continues to explore Philo's idea of the two stories of creation in Genesis. He develops the meaning of the two types of creation by highlighting the opposite natures of the two creators—the good and omnipotent God versus the jealous, counterfeit god. Although the Secret Revelation of John adjusts the stories to explicitly expose the cause and nature of evil, the similarities between Genesis and the Secret Revelation of John are also important. These similarities may be more subtle, but their fundamental premises are profound. Both texts understand the origins of evil to lie in action contrary to the knowledge and will of the true God. And both portray independent female thought and action as the cause of the disruption of harmony for humanity.

But significantly, the Secret Revelation of John shifts the blame for the work of evil away from human responsibility to forces not entirely under human control.[8] Sophia, for example, resided in the heavenly realm when she descended to the worldly darkness, bearing responsibility for the works of her offspring, Yaldabaoth. Other characters shift roles from Genesis too. Eve, according to the Secret Revelation of John, did not provoke sin in Adam but saved him from his mortal dream. Furthermore, in the Secret Revelation of John, Noah provides a way for all humans to be saved from the flood of the enemy instead of only his family and his animals. And finally, the beguiling powers of women came not from their own evil intents but from the seductions and the enticements of the counterfeit spirits.

For this reason, the second-century author of the Secret Revelation of John—dependent on Genesis and influenced by Platonic ideas and questions—depicts an image of humans who rely on the salvation of Christ as a transforming power, as a support to life—not as a judgment against it.

---

8. For a fuller analysis of the relationship between the Secret Revelation of John, Genesis, and Plato, see King, *The Secret Revelation of John*, 191–224.

In Chapter 3, we saw that the Secret Revelation of John retold the story of the creation of Adam and then embellished Eve's part in the garden of paradise with its own twist. Now we'll take a closer look at the retelling of Noah and the flood (Genesis 6–8). Here the author of the Secret Revelation of John focuses on understanding *why* the flood came to destroy humanity. Specifically, in Genesis 7:7 (NRSV), we read that "Noah with his sons and his wife and his sons' wives went into the ark to escape the waters of the flood." But in the Secret Revelation of John, the author thinks an ark is too small to contain all the goodness and authority of the divine power.

Noah had been warned (in both Genesis and the Secret Revelation of John) that the God/god who created humankind regretted having done so. Now he is preparing to destroy it by a catastrophic flood. If Moses, the presumed author of Genesis, wanted to convey the destruction of evil works and the safety of the God-ordained good, then the story of a flood (which was a common myth throughout the ancient world) was a vivid depiction of God's care for His/Her loved creation. With this the Secret Revelation of John appears to concur.

But according to the Secret Revelation of John, Moses's warning about a flood from "the enlightened majesty of Forethought" (Meyer, 130) was available to *everyone,* not just to Noah's family. In fact, more people than those who fit on the ark in Genesis were able to hide together in a bright cloud. It is clear that only those who heard the warning and still rejected the Savior's help would suffer in the darkness. The possibility of salvation for everyone reinforces the Savior's answer to John's sixth question, above. Even after everyone has been invited to join with those in the bright cloud, some reject their divine heritage and pay the consequences of their own decision.

In the Secret Revelation of John, Noah distinguishes the power of the Invisible Spirit from the counterfeit power of evil by exercising the all-embracing power of the Spirit and exposing the empty threat of the evil spirit. The Noah in Genesis could find safety only for his immediate family (and merely representatives of the animal kingdom). But the Noah in the Secret Revelation of John illustrates the value of the individual psyche (soul), who can make choices. This Noah made both options (salvation and destruction) available to the middle type of thinking (the psyche or the soul), so each soul either could turn to its spiritual resources for safety or could opt out of that care for the material side of life, which would result in ultimate darkness through the flood.

The Second Attempt: Rape the Women for Their Pleasure

Since Yaldabaoth failed to destroy most of the people through the flood, the first ruler plots again with his powers, but his second plan flops immediately. They attempt to send angels (evil spirits) to human women and raise their children entirely for their own pleasure. No explanation is given as to why this plan failed so quickly, but we might surmise that the women recognized the nature of these evil intents and rejected them.

The Third Attempt: Seducing Humanity into Darkness

> This time the evil spirits (called "angels") deceived the women first, through seduction. The angels changed their appearance to look like the partners of these women, and filled the women with the spirit of darkness that they had concocted, and with evil. They brought gold, silver, gifts, copper, iron, metal, and all sorts of things. They brought great anxieties to the people who followed them, leading them astray with many deceptions. These people grew old without experiencing pleasure and died without finding truth or knowing the God of truth. In this way all creation was forever enslaved, from the beginning of the world until the present day. (Meyer, 130)

Karen King's translation of the part where they are led astray reads: "And they beguiled the human beings who had followed them into great troubles by leading them astray into much error" (King, 25:12). Here it seems lies the extent of the sorrows of the human experience. Humanity has at last been beguiled by the evil and deceiving spirit. Desire, one of the four major passions, got control of human minds, and people followed its false pleasures "into much error." This is the great horror John had feared when he asked—in his sixth question to Jesus—what happened to people who voluntarily turned away?

From his previous five questions, John had been assured that everyone would be safely led to the light, because the "spirit of life" will descend, and everyone would be cleansed. Since no one can stand without this power, it comes to everyone. Even death will not prevent the safety of the soul. Those who have been led astray will be guided back. The transformation takes place by following the Spirit of Life, not by shrinking back into mortal origins.

But still, there are those who willingly turn away! Jesus had told John, "They will be taken to the place where the angels of misery go, ... [and] will be tortured and punished eternally" (Meyer, 129). This is just what happened when the evil spirits seduced the women to *voluntarily* follow the wrong path. At last they were completely deceived and "forever enslaved."

But wait! The Savior is coming, the Savior who knows deceit and knows the remedy. Christ is ever ready to battle the worst of the passions and to awaken the darkest and most remote thought, to lead from error to truth.

THE SONG OF VICTORY

Our narrator for the Secret Revelation of John yields center stage to the Savior, who now speaks for him/herself.[9] Telling the rest of the story in the first person, he/she relates exactly what happens and proclaims full victory. From the beginning of John's encounter with his Savior, it/he/she continually shifts into different forms, genders, and shapes. In this case, the Savior identifies herself as "Forethought" (*Pronoia: pro-noia*, meaning "fore-thought").

> Now I, the perfect Forethought of the All, transformed myself into my offspring. I existed first and went down every path. I am the abundance of light, I am the remembrance of Fullness. (Meyer, 131)

Forethought takes on the likeness of her human children and travels down every path in the realm of the great darkness so that she can enlighten the way for those who were lost. They don't recognize her, because the evil powers had made them forget their divine rights to the light.

So, Forethought enters again into the middle of the darkness, the middle part of the underworld, and brings with her the remembering that humans need in their imprisonment. But this time the foundations of chaos

9. This first-person account of the Savior's final act does not appear in the shorter of the two versions of the Secret Revelation of John. Whereas most scholars contend that the longer version consists of parts that were added to the original, shorter version, I think it is possible to consider the opposite—that the longer version was the original, and some of the text, including this passage, was later removed. It could have been expedient to remove sections that promoted a clearer message of healing, a critique against patriarchal society, and a stronger association with the "light of the world" as a link to the Gospel of John.

shake so violently, she fears the collapse will utterly destroy the humans before she can rescue them. She soars back to the root of her light until they are ready for the escape.

But she doesn't give up. For the third time, Forethought returns to the midst of darkness and the bowels of the underworld, restating her mission: "I am the light dwelling in light, I am the remembrance of Forethought" (Meyer, 131). Now she heads directly to the midst of humanity's prison, which is the prison of the body! But this battle is not fought between the Infinite Spirit and the human body, but between the Spirit of Light and the *counterfeit* spirit of the demons. The human body serves as the battleground on which light exposes the emptiness of darkness, and the fake power of demons yields to the true power of Spirit. Since Yaldabaoth never had any inherent power of his own, he tried to claim it by copying the only true power of the Invisible Spirit. Therefore, human bodies (battlegrounds for Spirit and Its counterfeit) never really exhibit the evil power of the enemy, even though they may seem to do so for a time. Complete purification from the impulses of demons—salvation itself—becomes evident in the body when the battle is over.

Here is where healing and salvation become closely intertwined. Darkness threatens all forms of life mentally, physically, and morally. When evil spirits are ejected from human consciousness, the body no longer suffers: mental agony leaves the soul, and so it is refreshed.

> I said, "Let whoever hears arise from deep sleep." A person wept and shed tears. Bitter tears the person wiped away, and said, "Who is calling my name? From where has my hope come as I dwell in the bondage of prison?" (Meyer, 131)

Whoever has suffered the pain and agony of feeling abandoned in suffering, helpless in pain, hopeless in sorrow, understands those tears. "Who is calling my name?" Who cares deeply enough about me to find me at the bottom of the pit? Who knows my suffering well enough to find me in the midst of chaos and destruction? Who has found the source of light? Do I dare hope for release from this prison of evil spirits?

What comforting words these must be to anyone who has lost hope:

> I am the Forethought of pure light, I am the thought of the Virgin Spirit, who raises you to a place of honor. Arise, remember that you have heard and trace your root, which is I, the compassionate. Guard yourself against the angels of misery, the demons of chaos,

and all who entrap you, and beware of the deep sleep and the trap
in the bowels of the underworld. (Meyer, 131–32)

We know what to do. Rise up. Remember what we have heard. Trace
our root back to the original knowledge we've been given of the realm of
the good. Guard against the suggestions of misery. Beware of the demons
of chaos, because that's the source of entrapment. Do not sleep and dream
the lies of the underworld. And besides all this, our honor has returned!

The Savior concludes her story:

> I raised and sealed the person in luminous water with Five Seals,
> that death might not prevail over the person from that moment
> on. (Meyer, 132)

To those enduring physical and mental torture, the promise of dramatic
rescue from the depths of despair is truly a gem worth cherishing. But why
would anyone want to be sealed in luminous water with five seals? Scholars
have not yet figured out the significance of five of them, but many agree
that "sealing" is a common term for water baptism among early Christ-followers. Whether baptism offers the means of protection or correction, the
ultimate promise is that death will never prevail. All forms of sin, sickness,
and death that would plague the human body and soul left to the control of
the demons have been met and mastered by the power of the divine Being.

THE SECRET REVELATION

The Savior now transforms from Forethought into Jesus. Still speaking in
the first person, he exclaims to John,

> Look, now I shall ascend to the perfect realm. I have finished ev-
> erything for you in your hearing. I have told you everything for
> you to record and communicate secretly to your spiritual friends.
> (Meyer, 132)

This is, after all, a secret revelation. It's a secret for two reasons. First, it is
John's responsibility to safeguard it. Whoever doesn't know its value may
trade it in for something less and would be cursed for doing so. The Savior
warns him, "Cursed be anyone who will trade these things for a gift, food,
drink, clothes, or anything like this" (Meyer, 132). Second, the revelation is
a secret hidden from those whose eyes are not ready to open. The Pharisee
Aramanios, who taunts John in the first place concerning his teacher, and

who suggests how Jesus had deceived him, claims that John's Master had filled his mind with lies and had turned John from the traditions of his ancestors. If he had listened to Aramanios, John never would have found the gems awaiting him.

These three gems may be difficult to find, and they are probably encased in ordinary-looking rock to the unaccustomed eye, but to those who are searching, they are beautiful beyond measure. First, the realm where the Infinite Spirit resides with all creation in harmony is always good and includes all power. This is an unshakable, unmovable fact. Second, the opposition to this realm is a counterfeit liar. Yaldabaoth and his authorities try everything imaginable to discount and destroy the continuity of good. But the third gem is the nature of the Savior who knows all the tactics of the evil spirits and supplies everything people need to know in order to awaken and remain alert to the wiles of the devil. Salvation is secure, bringing bodily health and wholeness to everyone who seeks it.

John had patiently waited for all three gems to be revealed to him. And after the Savior disappeared, he "went to the other disciples and reported what the Savior had told him." (Meyer, 132).

5

The Secret Revelation of John in the Twenty-First Century

The Secret Revelation of John was discovered just in time for the twenty-first century. It really was a *secret* revelation for a long time. Now is a good time to reveal the secret. When the 2020 pandemic swept over the world, millions of people got sick, lost jobs, and died. Before help could arrive, political tensions exploded like volcanoes: agony over systemic injustice flooded in like a tsunami, and anger erupted over senseless police brutality like a forest fire out of control. Fear spoke between masked and unmasked friends and neighbors, affirming that nobody was in control.

It could well have been a time like this when someone wrote the Secret Revelation of John. It's a message of hope for justice and healing. But why the big secret? If everybody needed help, why hide it? The secrecy could have something to do with the reason it has remained hidden in human history for so many centuries. While the Secret Revelation of John offered hope and healing for the majority of people, it also exposed the workings of a battle for power.

Even though John (the disciple in the story) was given instructions to write down this precious message and take it to his fellow disciples, the book was lost and buried. Scholars don't know why this once-popular book disappeared from the records of the Christian church. People may have just lost interest, but more likely it was intentionally removed from circulation.[1]

Readers could not miss the critique against false powers and control. Who would have been offended? For starters, we know that power-hungry world rulers (Roman authorities) ruled by fear through military campaigns, enslavement, and crucifixion, and the Secret Revelation of John offered ordinary people a new kind of freedom that the world rulers could not touch. Although we know the book is about demons and their control over the minds and bodies of people, oppressed people also knew this language was code for abusive Roman rulers. Demons and world rulers had significant similarities.

John's revelation held a secret key. It was the knowledge that the enemy power—whether demons or Roman authorities—was a complete fraud. It had no legitimate power, because it was only a counterfeit spirit. Like the fable of the emperor's new clothes, the rulers do not realize that their weakness has been exposed. Their downfall will be inevitable, and injustices will be addressed. Escape from the cruelty can become a possibility.

But the secret may have operated on multiple levels. It is doubtful that Roman rulers confiscated or banned the Secret Revelation of John, because it appears to have circulated widely until about the fourth century. What was going on then, centuries later, that would have contributed to the book's disappearance? The Secret Revelation vanished just around the time the Christian church leaders began to consolidate their own power. Constantine, the Roman emperor, had declared Christianity the true religion of the empire, and now Christian leaders occupied the same authority as their counterpart Roman rulers also held.

Would *they*—the new fourth-century Christian leaders—have banned the book? Surely the Secret Revelation of John couldn't have been regarded as a critique of the new Christian leaders, because there had been no such thing as a Christian church when it was written in the second century! Nonetheless, one could point to a fourth-century motive for silencing its message: holding power. The way John understood his revelation was that all power belonged to God, and that God bestowed this power on everyone.

---

1. Irenaeus of Lyon, one of the church fathers, left only small references in his writings for historians about the existence of the Secret Revelation of John. His agitated comments fit with his polemic views against similar teachings. But the fact the book was so well-known to Irenaeus in France, and that it wound up being copied and deposited in Egypt indicates at the minimum, a very wide distribution.

The hierarchical structure envisioned by John plainly undermined the royal patriarchal system of emperors, popes, and authoritative bishops.

Or, perhaps the book wasn't banned. It could have been highly prized by Christian monks who wanted to be buried with their precious texts. The Bedouin who claims he found what came to be called the Nag Hammadi collection while he was searching for fertilizer might not have wanted to admit that when the papyri turned up he was robbing a grave—which is where most Christian manuscript discoveries like this have been made. Whether banned or prized, the Secret Revelation of John (and other extracanonical texts from the Nag Hammadi library) appear to have been a preoccupation for many before they disappeared.

GOOD GUYS, BAD GUYS, AND OMNIPOTENCE

The struggle for power was not unique to the second century. Nor the fourth. Nor the twenty-first. Superhero flicks, westerns, spy thrillers, and other violent movies keep fascinating children and adults today, finding ever-new ways to tell the same story. The good guys use more violence to overpower the violence of the bad guys. But the good guys' violence is somehow good, and the bad guys' violence is bad. These stories, told through all forms of media to people of all ages, reinforce the common belief that violence works. When all else fails, violence used cleverly wins the day and empowers the good guys.

Is this because the good guys have the power to start with? Or is it because power transfers to the winners, who are now in a position to dominate, thus becoming the new good guys?

Walter Wink, a renowned theologian and biblical scholar, draws a direct link from the ancient Babylonian myth of 1250 BCE—long before the Secret Revelation of John—to our present attraction to violence.[2] He summarizes the story:

> In the beginning, according to the Babylonian myth, Apsu, the father god, and Tiamat, the mother god, give birth to the gods. But the frolicking of the younger gods makes so much noise that the elder gods resolve to kill them so they can sleep. The younger gods uncover the plot before the elder gods put it into action, and kill Apsu. His wife Tiamat, the Dragon of Chaos, pledges revenge.

2. Wink, *Powers That Be*, 45–48.

Terrified by Tiamat, the rebel gods turn for salvation to their youngest member, Marduk. He negotiates a steep price: if he succeeds, he must be given chief and undisputed power in the assembly of the gods. Having extorted this promise, he catches Tiamat in a net, drives an evil wind down her throat, shoots an arrow that bursts her distended belly and pierces her heart. He then splits her skull with a club and scatters her blood in out-of-the-way places. He stretches out her corpse full-length, and from it creates the cosmos.[3]

In this myth creation is depicted as an act of violence. Chaos (Tiamat) precedes order (Marduk). Evil precedes good, and the most violent god takes over all the power. Therefore, violence is the innate means by which humans maintain order. Wink goes on to explain that "the masses identify with the god of order against the god of chaos, and offer themselves up for the Holy War that imposes order and rule on the peoples round about."[4]

It is no different today, Wink explains. "Peace through war; security through strength: these are the core convictions that arise from this ancient historical religion, and they form the solid bedrock on which the Domination System is founded in every society."[5]

Wink's insights on what he terms "the Domination System" shed light on the power struggles going on within the story of the Secret Revelation, as well as what happened to it after it went public. Notice the historical evolution of the Domination System:

Prior to the domestication of the horse, plunder had been unrewarding, since one was forced to carry the loot on one's own back. The horse and the wheel suddenly made conquest fantastically lucrative . . . The numerical excess of females depreciated the value of all females, and the system of patriarchy was either born or sharply expanded.

No matter how high in the patriarchal social order a woman might rise, she was always controlled by men sexually and reproductively . . . Those in power created or evolved new myths to socialize women, the poor, and captives into their now-inferior status.[6]

3. Wink, *Powers That Be*, 45.

4. Wink, *Powers That Be*, 47–48.

5. Wink, *Powers That Be*, 48.

6. Wink, *Powers That Be*, 40–41.

Conquest continued to create new and higher classes, fostering a competitive drive to struggle for dominance. And given this, any society's greatest defense became taking on the characteristics of those who conquer. Now we recognize the spiral of violence.

Only the most violent can win—which brings us right up to the situation in the Secret Revelation of John as well as to the twenty-first century.

Who can stop the spiral? The first gem in the Secret Revelation of John becomes more precious as we realize its assigned role to end this evil spiral and domination. The first gem shows the supreme power of good, and when the *supremely* good guy (the One Infinite Spirit) wins, it no longer must compete.

This Deity in the Secret Revelation of John begins not from chaos but from order. When chaos erupts—with Sophia's descent to the human, psychical level—this Deity seeks no conquest, but to *save* everyone from the destructive elements of the violent Yaldabaoth.

Demons are the only enemy, not people. To exercise any power, demons have to deceive the gullible in order to gain control over their feelings and thoughts. In that way, jealousy, greed, fear, and so forth can harm them until the Savior rescues them and awakens them to find their own roots in the unshakable realm.

Omnipotence uses its supreme power, not to add to the spiral of violence, but to stop it and to empower good in everyone. All people in the order of this creation discover themselves to be good guys. Their goodness no longer slips into violence, because they have no domination to defend. Maybe omnipotence keeps it the way it was before horses were domesticated and wheels carried off others' fortunes.

Since the Secret Revelation of John is a book of liberation for women, for enslaved people, for all levels of society, and even for human bodies, this poses a problem for maintaining any hierarchical system besides the supremacy of the divine benevolence. In the Secret Revelation of John, we see both the divine and the Savior figures expressed in male and female terms. Eve is part of the salvation story for Adam, not a source of evil. And the true power derives from the divine Oneness, not from humans atop the patriarchal ladder.

And yet, there is no record of what actually happened to the Secret Revelation of John manuscripts in the fourth century. We know the patriarchal system of the Western Church continued to amass power for centuries.

And we also know that losers of battles are silenced. The Secret Revelation of John disappeared at about that time.

STILL HIDDEN IN
THE TWENTY-FIRST CENTURY

In a way, a third layer of secrets from John's revelation remains even to this day. Still, decades after the text was retrieved from an ancient jar or robbed grave(s) near Nag Hammadi, Egypt, in 1945, some would still prefer that the Secret Revelation of John remain hidden. Naturally, since history provided only a one-sided image of its story, scholars and Christians could easily imagine satanic forces lying dormant in those ancient codices. But once again, whatever the powers have been that tried to exclude and belittle the voice of the Secret Revelation of John, they don't hold water.

More recent scholarship is finding evidence that the category of religious texts labeled "Gnosticism" in the seventeenth century has no substantive meaning today. It is more accurately a linguistic tool for fending off whatever seems disruptive to a certain kind of Christianity, and whatever is called Gnosticism slips away from meaningful definition. When we strolled through an imagined second-century Alexandria (in the first chapter), we heard multiple teachers and philosophers searching for answers to life's difficulties. No voices of authoritarian power had yet been established to rule out other teachers and thinkers. Certainly we heard voices of disagreement, and even unbridled criticism. But the marketplace of ideas flowed with innovative insights. The Secret Revelation of John and other books came to be thought of as heretical centuries later, when Christians defined themselves more powerfully by designating that which they were *against*. But by the time the Secret Revelation of John was discovered another fifteen hundred years later, no one remembered what it really said. It was just something to be against . . . *until*, that is, twentieth-century people began to read it!

THE POWER OF HEALING

Now the plot thickens. There's more to it than religious doctrinal argument, or even the rebellion against government rulers and social injustice. The Secret Revelation of John unlocks the secret path to healing. Freedom for the physical body is extraordinary, not only for the wonderful physical peace it brings, but for the dominion exercised over the counterfeit controlling powers. Here is where the most vicious battle takes place: right at the central command station of the human being, in his or her psyche. To realize that every human has access to the powers over his own body is to confront the greatest of all powers in the cosmos.

But most of us are locked out of this secret, even though we read it with our own eyes. We have been duped by the counterfeit powers of modern living to believe we are helpless in the face of injustice and disease. We fight back, but we are not free. In fact, when confronted with the possibility that our psyche has the power to choose freedom, we are prone to become deeply offended. Knowledge of who we are and what we know is shaken to the core. We have the disadvantage of an education in Newtonian physics. We believe in a separation between body and spirit. In every age, though, some form of this secret reveals itself. Now, in the twenty-first century we have been given the capacity to move beyond those restrictions. Consider, for example, the possibilities of quantum physics.

QUANTUM PHYSICS

Modern studies in quantum theory push us beyond the reliability of our own senses or standard physics. And the possibilities in quantum physics bear a striking resemblance to the cosmology of our second-century text. People who are even a little familiar with quantum physics will recognize a strangely familiar phenomenon from the Secret Revelation of John: "his thought became a reality" (Meyer, 110). The basic idea in quantum physics is that at least *some* things depend on observation for their existence. This much is irrefutable. Despite our conviction in the laws of classical physics—mechanical events that involve forces acting on matter—the experiments in quantum physics are "stunningly successful. Not a single one of the theory's predictions has ever been shown wrong."[7]

What do we do with the irrefutable evidence that thoughts can govern action? In this age, we are only in the infantile stages of understanding this, and I want to emphasize that the current interpretations of quantum physics do not *prove* that all the data collected for its study are explained by quantum theory. Our interpretation of the data is still in question.

---

7. Rosenblum and Kuttner, *Quantum Enigma,* 5.

QUANTUM PHYSICS

Quantum physics answers questions and at the same time poses challenges for everyone, physicists and laypeople alike. It inspires new questions in almost any field of endeavor. The question it raises for readers of the Secret Revelation of John is whether or not these scientific discoveries might someday explain the possibility that God (Mind) is the sole source of true consciousness and action. Boiling it down to its simplest and most relevant statement about what quantum physics is, John Archibald Wheeler explains that "In the real world of quantum physics, no elementary phenomenon is a real phenomenon until it is an observed phenomenon."[8] Or even more simply, "Nothing is real unless it is observed."

The first gem we uncovered in the Secret Revelation of John revealed a particular view of God, the One Mind who is all loving and all-powerful, and who causes existence through *thinking*—or (we can say) observing. This powerful and loving God creates all true existence through the expression of God's Mind-Self. God's thinking creation into existence presents us with a key to health, freedom, dominion, and joy. We realize God is creating us.

However, experienced quantum physicists repeatedly warn that the link between physics and consciousness is still mysterious and is consequently susceptible to generating pseudoscientific nonsense. We cannot jump to conclusions that we now have the scientific proof of the truth of ancient wisdom. But the *possibilities* are here. Bruce Rosenblum and Fred Kuttner explain that "understanding the real *mystery* requires a bit more mental effort, but it's worth it."[9] Quantum mechanics may still be an enigma, but it is a science that cannot be ignored. It can motivate outrageous speculation, but it cannot be dismissed, because "quantum theory works perfectly; no prediction of the theory has ever been shown in error. It is the theory basic to all physics, and thus to all science."[10]

The fact that it tells us *something* about consciousness and interacts with the physical universe means that its implications are extremely relevant to a study of the Secret Revelation of John. We have learned that in the ancient text, when one is conscious of the presence of being, that presence cannot be measured. Furthermore, the act of measuring something (in time or space) removes it from the realm of the infinite idea. A brief history of the development of quantum physics will highlight its relevant aspects.

8. Wheeler, "Frontiers of Time," 10.

9. Rosenblum and Kuttner. *Quantum Enigma*, 9 (italics added).

10. Rosenblum and Kuttner, *Quantum Enigma*, 269.

A BRIEF HISTORY OF QUANTUM THEORY

First, Niels Bohr explained in the mainstream "Copenhagen Interpretation (1931)" that elementary particles do not exist until they are observed. He and his colleagues (Max Planck and Werner Heisenberg) argued that observation and matter are one. Planck said, "I regard consciousness as fundamental. I regard matter as a derivative from consciousness. We cannot get behind consciousness. Everything we talk about, everything we regard as existing, postulates consciousness."[11]

In their famous "EPR" (Albert Einstein, Boris Podolsky, and Nathan Rosen, 1935), Einstein and his colleagues questioned Bohr's assertions that quantum theory was consistent and its predictions would always be correct.[12] The whole idea troubled Einstein. "I like to think the moon is there," he quipped, "even if I am not looking at it." Yet he had to agree: "It is basic for physics that one assumes a real world existing independently from any act of perception—but this we do not *know*."[13]

Einstein sought to prove the existence of a world existing independently of its observation. He wanted to prove the incompleteness of quantum theory.[14] But it worked too well. His own discovery of the "spooky action at a distance" theory appeared to prove the immediate connectedness of everything, despite his own objection. He discovered how two elementary particles, though separated by a great distance, really have to be one, because the *viewing* of one causes the same thing to happen to the other.

John Bell later constructed an experiment to measure this *spooky* phenomenon[15] (later known as "entanglement"). But Bell's work led to two more strange possibilities: either (1) nothing is real at all but exists merely as a result of our perception, *or* (2) there is some influence that travels faster than light.[16] That is, the objects of our so-called physical world do *not* have their own independent existence, because particles depend upon *observation* or measurement for their being. Or else some influence operating faster than physical possibility accounts for the actions of things.

---

11. Sullivan, "Interviews with the Great Scientists," 17.

12. Rosenblum and Kuttner, *Quantum Enigma*, 159.

13. Rosenblum and Kuttner, *Quantum Enigma*, 166 (italics original).

14. Rosenblum and Kuttner, *Quantum Enigma*, 167–69.

15. In the 1970s, experiments were finally designed to test the mathematical theories, and in the 1980s Alain Aspect of Paris was actually able to perform the experiment, successfully verifying Einstein's original entanglement (or "instantaneousness") hypothesis.

16. Brooks, "Spooky Action at a Distance," 11.

OUR STRUGGLES WITH QUANTUM PHYSICS

The consistent *un*predictability of quantum mechanics requires that we use *abductive* reasoning in order to understand it. Like inductive reasoning, abductive reasoning is a form of logical inference which goes from an observation to a theory that accounts for the observation. But unlike inductive reasoning, abductive reasoning seeks the simplest and most likely explanation, despite human discomfort with its conclusions.[17] The discomfort in quantum physics is understandable, as even Einstein resisted the implications of his own discoveries.[18]

Our conventional wisdom, our worldview shaped by classical Newtonian physics, is challenged by quantum physics, because our worldview is fundamentally flawed. Instantaneous connectedness underlies the universe at its most basic level. However, Rosenblum and Kuttner argue that modern physics does not replace classical physics in the same way that the heliocentric solar system replaced a geocentric concept of it. They do affirm, though, that if you dig deep enough, you have either empirical facts (which are challenged by quantum mechanics) or consciousness to support the foundation of reality.[19]

Astrophysicist Laurence Doyle offers a degree of comfort, explaining that in fact the scientific revolution has already determined that it is *not* the evidence of matter but the evidence of *intelligence* that we generally agree is found to be superior and more reliable. For example, Copernicus used mathematics to reenvision the revolution of the heavenly spheres and persuaded others to change their *beliefs* based on these mathematical proofs, which contradicted the findings of the physical senses.[20]

Sir James Jeans, a pioneering physicist of the early twentieth century, suggested implications of these quantum discoveries many decades ago:

> The stream of knowledge is heading toward a non-mechanical reality; the universe begins to look more like a great thought than like a great machine. Mind no longer appears to be an accidental intruder

---

17. An example of abductive reasoning was Copernicus's choice between two theories that fit his data: either a design with complex planetary orbits that kept the earth at the center of the solar system, or the counterintuitive but simpler design of the sun at the center with simple planetary orbits. Abductively, he chose the far simpler design, even though the conclusion was far more difficult for human thought to acknowledge.

18. Brooks, "Matter of Interpretation," 16.

19. Rosenblum and Kuttner, *Quantum Enigma*, 242.

20. I am grateful to astrophysicist Dr. Laurance Doyle for granting me an interview on January 5, 2016, in which he shared these ideas.

into the realm of matter . . . we ought rather hail it as the creator and
governor of the realm of matter.[21]

However, if it is practicable that a causative power exists outside the
realm of material substance, then the possibility of a God/Mind being the
cause of existence is strengthened. At least it gives some plausible explanation for such phenomena as Jesus healing at a distance. A man had ap-
proached Jesus, begging him to come to heal his son, who was at the point
of death, but Jesus told him to return home, because his son would live
without Jesus needing to be there. On his way back, the father met with
his servants, who informed him of his son's healing, which occurred at the
same time Jesus promised it (John 4:46–54).

Werner Heisenberg, a theoretical physicist and pioneer in quantum
physics, recognized that

> Some physicists would prefer to come back to the idea of an objec-
> tive real world whose smallest parts exist objectively in the same
> sense as stones or trees exist independently of whether we observe
> them. This however is impossible.[22]

To reconnect with the second century, the Secret Revelation of John
helps us let go of our expectancy of physical measurements of time, space,
and the substance of *things,* since, of course, Newton had not yet presented
his theories. The ancient text provides a detailed account as to what it could
look like if we *did* abandon our expectations of classical physics. We would
be free to discover something more than "the same sense as stones or trees,"
because *things* behave in some kind of relationship to consciousness. "Its
thinking became a thing" (King, 5:13).

This freedom to see deeper and more broadly brings with it a profound
resistance, because the things we lean on for our worldview or our educated
security are taken out from under us. Our biggest difficulty is not so much
a loss of identifying stones as stones or trees as trees, but rather wondering
what happens to our *own* identity. How do we know who we are, if we don't
know what is real and what is not? When we discover the basic cause for
things coming from an entirely different source from what we have lived

---

21. Henry, "Mental Universe," 29.

22. Heisenberg, *Physics and Philosophy,* quoted in *Gaither's Dictionary of Scientific
Quotations,* 1738.

with, we tend to lose our bearings. We question our self-worth, because we no longer remain confident in what we know (or believe?) as truth.

WHOSE MIND?

With a clearer picture of mind as the cause and creator, we can see better how the psyche in the Secret Revelation of John is the source of identity and also becomes the seat of transformation. The psyche is that part of the human constitution that *chooses* which source of influence it will follow. Will it be the Mind that awakens spiritual consciousness? Or will it be the mind that puts people to sleep, causing them to forget their spiritual or divine heritage? The first gem in the Secret Revelation of John explains in great detail that the true origin of humanity comes about through the gazing power of the Infinite Spirit (Mind). Each idea (person) is established within the realm of the unshakable. One-third of the book is devoted to this idea, because it is so profoundly challenged by the opposition.

It's the demons (evil spirits) who wreak havoc. Working on the psyche, they try to seduce it, confuse it, and put it into a dreamy state where they can take control. When the demons succeed in gaining control over the psyche, their most important job is to make sure the victim forgets his or her own roots in the divine realm.

Yaldabaoth's demons (evil spirits) attempt to control everything relating to the condition of humanity—from managing the heat, cold, wetness, and dryness of the created atmosphere to creating and controlling every part of the human body, (fingers and toes, elbows and knees, sinews and sexual organs). Worst of all, the demons stir up passions—grief, pleasure, desire, and fear—in order to manipulate the psyche. As soon as a person agrees with the feelings of the passions—as if they are his or her own thoughts—then the passions are able to make that person sick. Their bodies follow the commands of the thoughts. Then people unwittingly identify with these false feelings, because they come through their own personal senses.[23]

It is true, as we saw in the Secret Revelation of John, that evil spirits sometimes fail, because the psyche is already too safely guarded by the true light. Those humans with guarded psyches are alert and cannot be fooled.

23. The fuller discussion of the demons and their specific control over all emotions and body parts is found in Chapter 3, in the section titled "Yaldabaoth's Creation of People" (p. 48).

But their successes at fending off the evil spirits only provoked the chief Evil Spirit (Yaldabaoth) to become more devious and sinister. Remember that as soon as Yaldabaoth realized that Adam was enlightened with Insight, he "threw him down into the lowest part of all matter" (King, 18:18) (where disease and death can destroy), but the "Epinoia of the light [a messenger from Spirit] who was with him [Adam] is the one who will awaken his thinking" (King, 19:15).

HOW DO WE KNOW WHAT'S REAL?

The Secret Revelation of John teaches why we should pay special attention to both the source of intelligence and the way we judge what is real. A kaleidoscope, shifting the view of its gems, reminds us that there are many angles from which to see things. Knowing these different angles helps us regain our bearings when we lose track of reality.

As we stand on earth observing the sun, our physical senses confirm that the sun is moving across the sky and around the earth. If we could stand on the sun and observe the earth, we would easily see that, indeed, it is the earth that is traveling around the sun.

Since we are unable to stand on the sun, however, we need to acknowledge the truth of math and science that disproves the report of our physical senses. Here is an example of where our physical senses must yield to a higher source of knowledge to *see* how the earth is moving relative to the sun. If we don't yield to this understanding, we will utterly fail in our attempt to send a spacecraft anywhere in the solar system.

In the same way, the Secret Revelation of John teaches that we humans can learn to *see* God differently from the way our senses report things. When humans try to conceive of God, or even the effects of God, through our personal knowledge, we tend to create, or imagine, a God in our own human likeness: a Father, Judge, or King (sometimes, even Santa Claus). But if we could observe the human condition from God's position—a task as impossible as standing on the sun, since we are *not* God—we should expect to perceive things from God's (Mind's) point of view. Mind/God, the Good, would naturally say, in the words of Genesis (1:27), I made you in *My* image and likeness. Again, the consequences are grave if we don't yield up the knowledge of our personal senses and learn to discern what the creating God knows. We will fail to experience the harmony of God's order and goodness if we try to live on our own without the guidance and care of Mind/God.

Here is where the Secret Revelation of John draws on Genesis again to back up its authority. It shows how God could create us in the "image and likeness of God." The author claims that the first Human is the "image of the Invisible Spirit" (King, 6:24), and that created beings "glorify the Invisible Spirit" (King, 9:14), implying their likeness to the Invisible Spirit. God/Spirit/Mind is telling us our true existence is a creation of, and reflection of, the divine Being. We're being guided to the way we can *see* from Mind's perspective. And if we fail to see from that perspective, we continue to suffer the delusion and experience the inevitability of God's opposite: sickness, sinfulness, and death.

Both the earth-and-sun relationship and humanity-and-God relationship show us the way opposites work. What we see from the earth is the precise opposite of the perspective from the sun. There is no blending of opposites. What the human brain imagines of God is also the opposite of what the central, creator Mind (God) "sees." Human perceptions come from a personal brain, rather than from the Mind of God (like the planet's "view" of the sun). Therefore, the mind that sets *itself* up as a creator and is not God necessarily perceives, or creates in his own mind, the opposite of what God (as Creator) sees or knows.

One thing has become clear as we put the pieces of the Secret-Revelation-of-John puzzle together: we have to change our standpoint and prepare for our own transformation to truly see the whole picture.

The majority of people today, particularly Christians, have learned to imagine God as King, Judge, or strict Father who passes judgment—and rewards and punishes accordingly. But the Secret Revelation of John conceives of God primarily as the great Mind, the cause of the life of the universe. These contrasting ideas of God result in strikingly different ways of thinking and living.

When people, even today, think of God as a Judge or King, they tend to strive for God's approval through correct interpersonal behavior. They know they must behave in their relationship with God and with other people to be worthy of the reward. When people think of God as Mind, they tend to seek insight and knowledge from this God, perhaps through meditation. *Understanding God and God's creation of other human beings in this way causes the realization of already being in the realm of harmonious action and wellness.* It is not a reward; it is a realization. Salvation from the King-God comes through obedience and agreement with established dogma, whereas salvation from the Mind/God comes through an understanding of and yielding to the thoughts of Mind. *Salvation* is probably not the right word in today's vernacular. But the concept is that we are safe from danger, free from evil influence, and whole in mind and body.

WHAT DOES MENTAL POWER HAVE TO DO WITH HEALING?

There was evidently a struggle with these ideas in antiquity just as there is today. It wasn't that everyone could see from God's point of view back then, and that eventually everybody changed their minds and were no longer able to see this way in the modern world. For instance, Plotinus, a third-century philosopher, argued long ago against the idea that the thoughts of people could actually influence their health! He was convinced that people got sick because of physical reasons: overwork, overeating, malnutrition, or decay. Sickness was a result of some specific physical law. He ridiculed his opponents for saying that "diseases are *daimonia* [demons] and they say that they are able to drive these out with words" (*Ennead* 2.9.14,14–16, quoted in Williams, *Rethinking "Gnosticism,"* 133). *Drive them out with words!* The idea of driving out a disease with words—or thoughts—was preposterous to the philosopher but not to the author of the Secret Revelation of John.

The mental connection is clear in the Secret Revelation of John (and for other thinkers of the time as well): Demons were everywhere and affected everyone, from the emperor on down to the lowest enslaved person. They could stir up the agony that comes from grief, pleasure, desire, and fear. Passions caused agitation, and agitation caused suffering. Demons were commonly thought to govern every portion of the body from the nose to the toes.

And the author of the Secret Revelation of John crashed through this stubborn law of victimization by waking people up from the mental dullness imposed on them by demonic influences. Just as Dorothy's dog, Toto, exposed the almighty wizard in the *Wizard of Oz*, so the Secret Revelation of John ripped off the façade of the supposed power of demons. Yaldabaoth was a fraud. His only power was to deceive, or trick, humans into believing the suggestions of his minions, the demons.

People don't believe in disease-causing demons anymore, though. Most people today are pretty convinced there aren't any little devilish beings that fly around and sneak into our bodies to make us sick. And yet we have to admit we don't know everything. Quantum physics convinces us of that now. We don't know why evil things happen. What makes some people sick but not others? What makes us lose our bearings? In quantum physics, the cause of motion still operates at the level of minuscule particles. But the idea that thoughts affect things awakens us to greater possibilities for the mind than we had been willing to consider before.

We no longer fear little creatures who might invade our minds and bodies, but have we fully understood the ramifications of mental influence on bodies and souls? Flash mobs, advertising, social media, and even school spirit or corporate ethos remind us that we live in a world of influences. So, in lieu of using the term "demon," we can continue speaking with relevance for today by imagining these evil influences as "evil spirits."

For the author of the Secret Revelation of John, the Savior appeared in multiple forms and performing the office of thought-messenger sent from God. This Savior was not a named person, but as John recognized him in the opening scene of the Secret Revelation of John, this Savior was first a child, then an old person, and finally a servant. The author clarifies for his readers that "these semblances . . . were not multiple beings but there was only a single likeness having many forms" (King, 3:8). Later, when this Messenger/Savior comes to awaken those who had been imprisoned in their bodies, she comes in a female figure with multiple names and missions.

The power of this Savior lay in the truth, because it exposed the supposed power of disease, sin, and suffering as a fraud. Just as the view from the earth to the sun mirrors the opposite of the facts of sun to earth, the sense of discord and destruction mirrors the opposite of the truth of God's relationship to creation.

Bodies governed by passions and the cruel control of demons all came from the counterfeit spirit, a jealous god. Deceitful and angry, the Chief Demon (who today could be called Satan or Evil Spirit) craved the power of the real God. He/It was willing to destroy all creation to get it. But discerning the motives and methods of this enemy, the all-powerful and all-loving God sent a Savior to awaken everyone who had been deceived and had lost their way.

A TRANSFORMATIONAL EXPERIENCE

This ancient text was never meant to be a scholarly theory or museum artifact. It was written from the heart, to heal a broken heart. In the opening scene, John lays bare his emotional distress: "I grieved greatly in my heart" (King, 2:7). The appearance of this Savior comforts him, but the comfort he comes to offer is about to change every aspect of his life. He is about to be shaken awake so that he can find his way home.

Just as quantum physics shifts the locus of action from the observed object to the observing subject, so the action in the Secret Revelation shifts for John from the object to the subject. That is, John discovers how *he*— as the subject—can make the shift from a sufferer to a voice of authority. This shift would have been a shock to anyone living in the tightly ordered, hierarchical world of the second-century Mediterranean. There, authority typically descended through lines of patriarchal power and was never given to an individual to act on his or her own! In quantum physics as we understand it today, the observer (the subject)—and not the thing observed (the object)—controls the situation. But the implications of this come as a shock to many living in the Western world, even to those with a general education in science.

The shift from object to subject occurs in both the Secret Revelation of John and in quantum physics because action is found to be caused by a mental source, not by impersonal physics or something beyond our range. We have yet to see how much emotion will be detected in the action of quantum physics, but in the Secret Revelation of John, the mental source (Mind of God) creates a comforting and peace-giving place for John to be. In that sense, quantum physics might serve only as a metaphor, shifting our view from the object (external things happening to us) to the subject (our causing things to happen). In quantum physics, *observation* causes movement.

But in the Secret Revelation of John, "gazing" causes more than the motion of a single object. It causes all of creation to come about. For John, the shift to a different source of action causes a complete transformation for him—of body and soul. For the physicist, the shift from the cause-and-effect of classical physics to the power of the observer represents a complete transformation in understanding the universe as well.

Whether the Secret Revelation of John and quantum physics are related more than metaphorically will be determined sometime in the future when both are more fully understood. But for now, the value of pausing to consider the ramifications of quantum physics lies in its ability to move modern thinkers beyond their disbelief in mental causes. We should expect a real transformation to change our convictions to a higher consciousness, and a better mind and body will become apparent.

THE PSYCHE (HUMAN MIND) CAN BE RESCUED

The psyche's roots in the divine realm never disappear. Each male and female (made in the image and likeness of God) retains roots in the unshakable realm, even when the evil spirits succeed in temporarily deceiving a person. The Savior maneuvers and comes to the rescue in surprising and unexpected ways because she knows the tactics of her enemy. *She/He knows exactly what the psyche needs to counteract the influence of the counterfeit spirit's deceitful nature.*[24]

To the psyche, the rescue feels like an awakening. Everything changes. Healing happens, because the psyche realizes a whole new outlook, a deep transformation of body and soul. According to quantum physics, particles change—or move—according to a thought change. Stories in the Secret Revelation of John demonstrate how bodies can change—or be healed—according to a thought change.

When the perfect Pronoia (Forethought) came as one of the forms of the Savior to rescue suffering people, she "traveled into the vastness of the dark" (King, 26:5), but these were not dead people she came to rescue. These were people who had been manipulated by the evil spirits and had succumbed to the passions. Their lives were nearly destroyed. She entered into "the midst of their prison, which is the prison of the body" (King, 26:21). And she describes her encounter with those she has come to save. She calls out,

> "Whoever hears, arise from lethargic sleep!"
>
> And he [a prisoner] wept, shedding tears; heavy tears he wiped from himself. And he said "Who is it who calls my name and from where does this hope come to me who am dwelling in the fetters of the prison?" (King, 26:22–25)

---

24. Such gender blending is common throughout the Secret Revelation of John. At times the Savior is "she," and at other times the Savior is "he."

Pronoia introduces herself as the *thought* of the virginal Spirit, the one who raises the sufferer to "the place of honor" (King, 26:27). Then she describes what happened next:

> And I raised him up and sealed him [baptized him] with the light
> of water with five seals so that death would not have power over
> him from this day on. (King, 26:32–33)

If people are rescued so that death has no power over them, they are still living. But they are no longer imprisoned in their bodies, because demons have no more control. "Fortify yourself against the angels of poverty and the demons of chaos, and all those who ensnare you," Pronoia warns, "and be watchful of the lethargic sleep and the garment of the inside of Hades" (King, 26:30–31). As we read this moving account of the rescue in the twenty-first century, we certainly run across ideas that bear no resemblance to our current world. But we can't miss the ideas that endure. We do not need to stretch our imagination to appreciate the importance of fortifying ourselves against the angels of poverty and the demons of chaos.

As the story continues, Pronoia has reached the psyche. "Beware," she encourages the people she came to help. "Don't let the evil spirits mess around with you. Stay on your guard, and think your own thoughts!" This is a contemporary paraphrase, of course, but it illustrates how relevant this warning can be for people today who may be confronted with a spirit of depression or negativity. Denying the good already present is exactly what the evil spirit seduces us to do. The suggestion—always a suggestion—whispers, "Never take that first gingerly step to be fully Human, to be free."

But most of all, the Savior inspires a promise of hope and restoration. In the form of Pronoia or Forethought, she announces that she is light in the darkest darkness who comes to break the bondage of despair. In the form of a spirit sent by the Lord, he awakens the sick and suffering from forgetfulness, and they receive knowledge.

Why is knowledge such a valuable gift from the Savior? When we investigated the meaning of the first gem, early in the Secret Revelation of John, we learned how highly prized *gnosis* would be. This is the knowledge of God that banishes evil spirits. But this God does not line up with the King-Judge-Father image most modern Christians have imagined. This is the Mind/God who knows us, caused us to be who we are, and loves us. This Mind/God who caused us to exist also enables us to *know* who we are.

In profound darkness, the Savior searches for us and finds us. She provides the knowledge of who we are as God's likeness. No wonder John asked so many questions about this kind of saving! "Will *all* psyches be led safely to the pure light?" "What about those who rejected the *gnosis*?" "Will it be different when the soul (psyche) leaves the body?" The psyche is where decisions are made. Will I follow the light? Will I be distracted by counterfeit enticements? The psyche is where the body is governed too, since the body doesn't act on its own. The body is governed either by evil spirits (the counterfeit spirit) telling us we know nothing, or by the spirit of light telling us that we know the truth. Knowing! Knowing God is knowing ourselves. Knowing ourselves, we know we are free, whole, and reflecting the light of the divine.

IS THIS REAL HEALING OR MERELY FANCY?

The best protection against invasion from evil spirits is the *gnosis* (knowledge of God's truth) about one's own enduring identity. This knowledge guards thought from being controlled unwillingly, and it lifts the veil on the mind already manipulated. Conscious awareness of Mind's/God's control feels like health or healing, because the physical body corresponds to whatever is controlling the psyche.

Numerous thinkers have tried to make sense of the phenomenon of non-physics-driven healing. The Secret Revelation of John was written before anyone knew anything about DNA, germ theory, or biomedicine. And yet, the "fingerprints of God"[25] continue to appear to the faithful and skeptical alike. People from around the globe and throughout human history continue to recount firsthand experiences of the restoration of health without medical explanation. From time to time, even medically trained doctors agree these healings occur as described, contrary to medical law. Some write off these healings as due to the placebo effect. Some consider them instances of the paranormal. Even in Jesus's day, people often dismissed them as magic.

But the three gems of the Secret Revelation of John, polished and buffed for modern viewing, remain before us as a consistent and logical gift for anyone willing to experience the transformation that they cause. It is a reasonable argument that God would be good and omnipotent, that evil would be a counterfeit force, and that healing would be an inevitable element of salvation. *But this possibility can only be experienced if we're willing*

25. The title of Hagerty's book aptly describes the phenomenon of God's healing presence and action indescribable through medical law: *Fingerprints of God*.

to change. Changing a point of view can be as simple as listening to the other side of an argument. Or it can involve profound change of heart.

More often, we refuse to consent to the idea of an omnipotent God. Believing in an all-powerful God seems to imply that we are turning our backs on real people who are suffering, and that we are pretending the suffering is a mere illusion! What decent person could follow a God who would allow blatant cruelty and suffering in all corners of the world today? The Holocaust slammed the door shut on the static and dominant image of God. This god of the counterfeit world was not there for the six million Jews! These serious issues bring us face-to-face with the problem of God.

Either we will hold our ground in solidarity with the suffering and dying, or else we will consider a type of transformation that leads to life in the presence of sorrow and pain. The Savior offers a provocative example. She struggled to find and be with those who were in the depths of darkness. This compassion could be a form of solidarity. But she neither left them there nor stayed with them there. She was the force for light, or life, and removed them from the unjust imprisonment. Her powers for good were great enough to overwhelm any form of opposition. No lesser power could have done it.

In fact, this is where we met John the disciple at the beginning of the Secret Revelation of John. All his hopes and expectations had evaporated when Jesus was captured and shamefully crucified. And with that unjust horror, hope vanished for everyone. The Savior (messenger from God) came to John in the depth of his prayer, and the Savior explained how John could awaken to life so that he could see the goodness of God's realm.

But even with the first and second gems—those logical explanations of a good and omnipotent God—John's first questions turned to his concern for everybody else. Does everybody get saved? What happens if some don't change their ways and follow the light of life? The beauty of the third gem opened for John the conviction that everyone *can* be helped. But he learned from the Savior's teaching that he could not help anyone else if he remained asleep in the same prison.

The images of the earth-centered and sun-centered systems help us to reframe the question. If we had tried to send a rocket from earth to another planet *without* changing our view of the sun's relationship to the earth, we would have miscalculated the direction of the other planet, and the rocket would never have arrived at its hoped-for destination.

It must have been painfully difficult to convince people that the sun was not moving in relation to the earth, when *everyone knew* for certain that the sun rotated around the earth. Everybody could see it. But in fact, they had it all wrong! The earth was doing the moving. It is painfully difficult to convince ourselves that we might be wrong about anything.

But this pain is a wounded ego. Biblical language may sound too archaic, and we resist "taking up our cross" to follow the light. Self-immolation sounds too Victorian for the self-confident worldview of the twenty-first century. But who needs to yield? Will we choose an all-powerful, loving Mind/God, or will we stay with the mind-ego apart from God? The Savior found John at the point of vulnerability. His wounds opened his heart to hear and to change.

CONCLUSION

The Savior who came to John from God knew his pain, knew his incredulity, and knew that John would need thorough transformation to see the presence of good right then and there. So the Savior presents us (the readers) with powerful questions to ponder: Will we choose to argue on the side of death, pain, and sorrow? Or will we choose to argue on the side of life and the continuity of good? This is the work of the psyche. Which will it be?

These questions are still here today. If we choose the side of good, what happens to those who are suffering? Will they have what they need? According to the Savior in the Secret Revelation of John, if we are willing to disagree with our own feelings, our educated beliefs in physics, and our conviction in the supremacy of evil, we will discern and experience—at least to some degree—the power of good that heals and breaks the jaws of evil.

To be certain of the fruition of John's full transformation at the end of the book, the Savior leaves him with final instructions while he departs again for the perfect realm.

> I have finished everything for you in your hearing. I have told you everything for you to record and communicate secretly to your spiritual friends. This is the mystery of the unshakable generation. The Savior communicated this to John for him to record and safeguard. He said to him, "Cursed be anyone who will trade these things for a gift, for food, drink, clothes, or anything like this." These things were communicated to him in a mystery, and at once

the Savior disappeared. Then John went to the other disciples and reported what the Savior had told him. (Meyer, 132)

Here I offer a twenty-first-century paraphrase:[26]

> The healing messenger finished saying what we need to hear within the depths of our being. We have been told everything so that we can give to anyone else who is willing to hear. It will appear as a secret to those who close their ears. The promise of unshakable peace is a mystery for those who will not look more deeply. We treasure this awakening and commit to preserving it for all humanity. We would be cursed to the depths of our being if we exchanged this gift from God for any type of earthly pleasures and glory. These things come in the purity of heart-to-heart prayer with God. Then the presence leaves us, and we can go out to share it freely with anyone willing to hear.

This is the secret revelation that came to John—who preserved these gems for the millennia to come. Even when people have died in a pandemic, when political tensions have exploded like volcanoes, when agony over systemic injustice floods in like a tsunami, and anger erupts over senseless police brutality like a forest fire out of control, the message remains that our eyes can be opened. The choice is still before us. If we are willing to listen, look, and welcome our own transformation, then we will be prepared to give what we have been given. We will be ready to see the way out toward a life prepared for everyone by an all-powerful and good God.

---

26. See my complete paraphrase of the Secret Revelation of John in Chapter 6 of this book.

6

A Paraphrase of the Secret Revelation of John

*R*eading the Secret Revelation of John even in English translations is not easy. But as many extraordinary gems are encrusted with layers of unsightly rock, the gems in this text are worth the patient polishing process. Some readers may find it easier to approach the text by reading this book first with its cultural setting and explanations for contemporary perspectives.

Others may prefer to start with the text itself, to get a feel for what the Secret Revelation of John is all about. Unlike the text itself, this paraphrase is presented almost as a stage play with character voices identified. The purpose is to help readers keep track of who is speaking while maintaining the intent and meaning of the text as much as possible.

Those who read this paraphrase first may find the flow of the preceding book easier to follow when they turn to it, and of course those who have read the book first will find the meaning of the text more easily when they come to this paraphrase.

CHAPTER 1[1]

Narrator: Here is the teaching of the Savior, along with the explanation of the mysterious things that he taught his disciple John. This John is the

1. For ease of usage, this paraphrase follows the chapter delineations of King's

brother of James, and they were known in biblical times as the sons of Zebedee.

CHAPTER 2

Narrator: One day, after Jesus has been crucified, John is on his way to the temple, when Arimanios, a Pharisee, approaches him. He is clearly still quite aggravated about Jesus and how he had disrupted the traditions, so he taunts John with cruel questions.

Arimanios, the Pharisee: Where's your teacher now? The one you trusted and followed?

John, the disciple: He returned to the place he came from. That's all I can say about it.

Arimanios, the Pharisee: That nobody from Nazareth fooled all of you disciples. He told you lies and closed your minds. And now you've even lost your connection with your Jewish roots!

John, the disciple: When I (John) heard this, I turned my back to the temple and headed to a quiet place in the hills. My heart pounds, and my grief nearly overwhelms me. I have questions too! Why did his heavenly Father send him into the world? Who *is* this Father? Does he give us any clues to what happens to the rest of us after this world comes to an end?

I'm trying to remember what he said about this. He said there's another place, not like this, because it's indestructible, but he didn't really say anything more about it. What is it like? Are we really alone? What is the connection between where he is and where we are?

CHAPTER 3

John, the disciple: Right when I am in the depth of my thoughts, I see something far beyond the reaches of the sky. The whole earth has become illuminated, and everything begins to shake like an earthquake.

I'm terrified. Am I beginning to see something of the connection between that divine place and the earth? A young child comes up next to me, as if from nowhere. But as I take a closer look, I realize he is apparently an old person. And then he changes again, looking more like a servant. I'm not

---

translation, but the paraphrase is mine.

talking about multiple people. Standing in what seems like a spotlight, it is easy to see this is one being, but I'm quite conscious that this person is able to be multiple forms. Each image shines through the other, as if all three aspects of this person are important for me to see.

And he speaks directly to me, asking so earnestly,

Teacher/Lord/Savior/Jesus: John, John, why are you doubting? Why are you so afraid? You're not a stranger to this. You have learned to see beyond the surface of things, and you know who I am. I'm here to help you. You remember how often I told all of you, "I am the one who is with you always, at all times, and under all circumstances."

When you see me, you see the heavenly Father. Also, when you see me, you see the heavenly Mother. And so, likewise, when you see me, you also see the heavenly Son. That's why I am always with you. You can recognize me for who I really am, because nothing has ever defiled me.

Now I have come to teach you what you are ready to hear and understand. You will see what has come into being, what's here now, and what will come into being, because you can understand both the things that are visible and invisible. This is essential for understanding the continuity of good.

Nothing will shake your faithfulness, because you will be able to discern perfection from every angle.

Prepare yourself to hear what I have come to teach you today. As you take it all in, you will be ready to explain it to your friends. They also will come to realize their innate loyalty and trustworthiness.

CHAPTER 4

John, the disciple: I tell him I'm ready. I want to understand. So, he launches into the full explanation about the place he came from, why evil could come about despite the continuity of goodness, and how the power of good dispels the counterfeit nature of evil.

The Perfect Realm of Being

Teacher/Lord/Savior/Jesus: John, there is one God, and I want you to ponder the depth and breadth of what this means. Try to imagine the greatest monarchy above this God, and it is impossible, because there is no king or kingdom with more power and authority. Now imagine this same God as the Father of all that exists. The things that you see and the things that you don't see—they are all fathered by this One.

Let's consider the meaning of infinitude. You cannot see this One Father of all existence, because everything about this One is infinite—beyond what the human eyes can see. The same is true concerning absolute purity. This One mixes with nothing else, and none of your human senses can experience such perfect purity. All light emanates from this infinitude and purity, and this light counteracts the slightest corruption of darkness.

Now try to compare this Oneness with any other kind of god you've known. Let's call it Invisible Spirit, and you can realize why there is no other kind of god that can overpower, outshine, or outwit infinite Invisible Spirit.

Consider what it means to be eternal. It's more than a long time, because It is the unstoppable continuity of good. Since It persists in perpetuity without needing any assistance, It contains within Itself total perfection. Its inextinguishable light reveals Its goodness forever.

Can you think of anything that could limit it? No! It is inconceivable, because no one existed before Its eternal existence. Our own limitations limit us, not the eternal good.

You can't even *measure* the continuity of good, because no one can find a starting place to measure. For the same reasons, our human vision cannot behold It. Eternity exists within Itself, and our human limitations cannot hold it within our grasp.

Can you imagine a proper name? No, because our language isn't big enough to grasp all of the Oneness. So, let's consider this again: We're talking about immeasurable light that cannot become contaminated, the continuity of good. It can't even exist in human images of perfection, blessedness, or even divinity, because Its eternal goodness always extends beyond the human concept.

You have to remove the idea of corporeality in order to grasp the idea of this God. You can't even think of *in*corporeality, because you can't start with the notion of corporeality to find the substance of God. That's why the concepts of large and small don't even apply. It's impossible to measure by any known quantity.

In fact, it's easier to describe the fullness of God by noting all the human measurements you *can't* use. Since the human mind simply cannot circumscribe it, how could we define It from our limited perspective? Considering its completeness, how could it ever participate in realms defined by the limitations of time or space? Imagine this: if it participated in such a finite realm, something preceding it would have had to prepare for it. Impossible! How could it receive something from anything else? It would have experienced insufficiency before it received anything, and It has never been deficient.

As we try to wrap our thought around this vast Allness, we recognize that Oneness causes the only true knowledge of Itself, and Its light illumines Its own marvel. And, as light brings out Its full nature, It radiates life, blessing, understanding, and goodness. It may feel to us, in our finite ways, as if It gives us mercy and salvation. This is the way grace works—it is not a possession of the Infinite One, but Its grace gives where we can be conscious of it.

CHAPTER 5

Teacher/Lord/Savior/Jesus: I need to explain more about this light even though it is so difficult to comprehend. Like the Oneness from which it emanates, this light is indestructible and exudes infinite power. There is no power than can agitate this light in the slightest. Pure stillness defines its mightiness, but this great power is not static. Its goodness causes it to *give* its strength to all, just as the light beam gives its light.

Narrator: The only one who can really explain these things with authority is the one who has come directly from the Father. This is the way we learn how the Father—or, the *One*—causes existence to be.

Creation Comes into Being

Teacher/Lord/Savior/Jesus: He gazes at Himself in the pure light, which is also the source of living water. This conscious reflection in the light and water is the reality that the One wants. Or, we could say that in this way His thinking actually becomes the reality by reflection.

Then a female presence comes forth directly from His thought, in the presence of this shining, reflecting light. Her light and power also exude from Her presence, because She is the image of the perfect and Invisible Spirit. She is Barbelō, the perfect female complement to the Father. She praises this Spirit from which She had come and establishes forever the loving and praiseworthy relationship between Creator and creation. For this, She becomes the universal womb. Every father-mother, every human, the holy Spirit, and all forms of being emanate from this nourishing source of life.

CHAPTER 6

Teacher/Lord/Savior/Jesus: In Her loving relationship with the Father, Barbelō—also known as Forethought (Pronoia)—asks for important characteristics for the fullness of creation. She recognizes what is needed to nurture and protect all creation. The Father ("Invisible Spirit") agrees and gives Her everything She needs, and in the same manner that She also had appeared. That is, these are the Father's thoughts that become reality: foreknowledge, incorruptibility, eternal life, and truth. All of them take after Barbelō and love to praise both the Spirit-Father and Barbelō. All of the Father's thoughts came into being because of Barbelō's forethought.

CHAPTER 7

Teacher/Lord/Savior/Jesus: Everything is in place, and now the foundation for the fullness of creation has been laid. We'll see how the male and female ideal work together in oneness. The Father gazes into Barbelō with the same pure light in which He looks at Himself, and She conceives. They reflect the great goodness together, and their mutual awareness of it results in begetting a spark of light resembling the original source.

This only-begotten offspring inspires rejoicing and nurturing from the Parents who raise him to the point of perfection. When he is ready, this only direct descendant comes to stand in the presence of the Invisible Spirit who anoints him with goodness. Immediately upon his anointment, he glorifies the holy Spirit and the Forethought. After all, it was through Forethought that he had been revealed! This generation of offspring took place without physical involvement, but their relationships are secure in goodness and mutual appreciation.

In the same way Barbelō had known the necessity of foreknowledge, incorruptibility, eternal life, and truth, the anointed Son realizes what's needed to fulfill the reasons for being. He puts in a request to the Invisible Spirit for a fellow worker who should be Mind. By the same means of creating—through looking into the light—the fellow worker (Mind) appears as a revelation of the Invisible Spirit. Working right with the anointed Son, Mind wishes to create by means of the Invisible Spirit's word, so that everything is given meaning. The Son now has become the anointed expression of all being. Having originated from the Invisible Spirit, being conceived by the Mother, and at one with the Mind, the anointed Son is now equipped with the understanding to generate from Himself and with the ultimate authority of truth.

CHAPTER 8

Teacher/Lord/Savior/Jesus: Light is becoming ever more creative and meaningful. One of the most beautiful ideas of the Son was to cause the light to reflect back to the One through a prism of four lights. All the lights magnify important characteristics of the fullness of Being. Don't think people originate these things. People aren't even created yet! The prism magnifies the meaning of the light, clearly showing how they include

First: grace, truth, and form

Second: insight, perception, and memory

Third: understanding, love, and idea

Fourth: perfection, peace, and wisdom.

CHAPTER 9

Teacher/Lord/Savior/Jesus: All creation comes into being so that the One can be glorified! This is what the Invisible Spirit wants. Goodness should be realized, appreciated, remembered, and loved with grace, and this is the great cause of existence. The anointed Son of the One and the Mother made it happen.

What's needed next is the perfect Human, ready to activate the whole heavenly plan. Adamas is that perfect Human and is able to put it all into action through the grace, truth, form, insight, perception, memory, understanding, love, idea, perfection, peace, and wisdom already prepared for him. With these twelve characteristics, Adamas is fully prepared to glorify God to the fullest.

But Adamas is not at all like the type of human who thinks he can originate good or bad by himself. This perfect Human dwells with the anointed Son and consequently has an invincible power of mind. Adamas's first act is to praise the great Creator.

Adamas: Because of you, Invisible Spirit, everything has come into being!
And to you everything will return.
I praise you and glorify you and your self-creating son.
You three are the perfect power: Father, Mother, and Child.

Teacher/Lord/Savior/Jesus: Reflecting the One's love for all creation, Adamas fathers a child named Seth. Like Adamas, who has authority over the first light, Seth is bestowed with authority over the second light.

And so the multiplication of light continues. Next, all the offspring of Seth are appointed over the third light. They fully embrace and reflect the great light and glorify the abundance of good.

And the fourth light embraces everyone, even those who just can't grasp it all at once. They are patiently supported until they are ready to take it all in. As they turn in repentance from their limitations, they discover that they have belonged all along to the place prepared by the Spirit of goodness.

CHAPTER 10

Teacher/Lord/Savior/Jesus: Wisdom is one of those characteristics predicted by Forethought to be an essential component of the heavenly realm. Wisdom is also such a key element in the unfolding of the living universe that it also takes on a personified form using the Greek term for "wisdom"—*sophia*—for her name. Within the normal order of the realm, male and female partners are inseparable, but Sophia conceived an idea and deliberated it without the will and understanding of Her male partner.

But Her invincible power and pursuit of a will apart from unity with the male produces an offspring unlike its mother. Here is the first hint of the special relationship between the divine goodness and the misshapen ugliness of mortality. Sophia (wisdom), an inhabitant of the realm of God, will be called upon to sort out the difficulty.

Where Evil Comes From

Teacher/Lord/Savior/Jesus: Sophia had wanted something that was inconsistent with the natural order of male and female unity, but the enactment of her ignorant willfulness causes her to produce a monster.

She herself becomes appalled at the repugnant appearance of such an outcome. She beholds his powerfully enraged face that resembles a lion and his deceptive nature like a slithering serpent. His eyes shoot out lightning toward her, and she knows she has to get rid of him. She names him Yaldabaoth and knows there is no place for this deformity in the light of harmony.

CHAPTER 11

Teacher/Lord/Savior/Jesus: The repulsive reaction is mutual. Yaldabaoth also withdraws from the place where he had been born, and he creates for himself his own kingdom in a blaze of fire. Dazed by his own madness, he produces his own kind of false powers and authorizes them to act in his name. These powers are also called "rulers" or "authorities," because Yaldabaoth wants to maintain control over his whole realm through this enactment of power. There are twelve powers with names like Cain, Abel, and Belias (the one who presides over Hades).

Then Yaldabaoth sets up seven kings over their own heavens. And five more kings preside over the depth of the abyss. These kings differ a bit from the powers/rulers/authorities, because the kings maintain authority over the heavens and the abyss, whereas the other powers are assigned authority over the human situation.

CHAPTER 12

Teacher/Lord/Savior/Jesus: In the darkness of his own ignorance, Yaldabaoth divides his fire among the kings, but he gives them no light from his mother. It's remarkable that when light mingles with darkness, light emerges. But when darkness mixes with light, the light just becomes dim. This is the nature of Yaldabaoth. He is weak, like the dim light, because he tries to create from the basis of darkness. Everything he wants to do is a reversal of all that his mother gave him. He blasphemes, when everything else is glorifying God.

Yaldabaoth (Chief Demon/Ruler): But listen to me! I am God, and no other god exists except me!

Teacher/Lord/Savior/Jesus: As the mirror opposite of the One, Yaldabaoth tries to imitate the One Invisible Spirit, but he is fully ignorant of the origin of his strength.

So his rulers/authorities/powers begin propagating on their own—seven more powers for themselves. And each of these seven powers creates six angels until—between all of them—they have produced 365 angels, who in turn can control every day of the year! Now, these angels (also known as "demons") have direct power to control parts of people's lives.

Furthermore, all seven of the original powers take direct control over one day of the week. Each one has an animal-like face: a sheep's face, a donkey's face, a hyena's face, a serpent's face (with seven heads), a regular serpent's face, a monkey's face, and a fiery face that shines. But Yaldabaoth has more faces than all of them put together. With these faces, he maintains his superiority by showing himself in front of all of them in any face he wants.

CHAPTER 13

Teacher/Lord/Savior/Jesus: His attempts to mix darkness with light begin to look increasingly like the human situation with a jumble of good and bad states of thought. Yaldabaoth is now willing to share some of his fire with his fellow authorities/powers. But because of the light from his mother, he retains his lordship over all of them. In fact, in demonstration of his arrogance, he calls himself God, and defies his origins.

But he still wants to put some of the glory that belongs to heaven into the grasp of each of his authorities/powers. So he conceives of various combinations, and they come to pass. For example, he pairs goodness with the first authority, Athouth (the sheep's face). Forethought, divinity, lordship, kingship, zeal, and intelligence are paired up with the others.

Why? Not to give them hope for a good future, but for the purpose of destroying them. It's their dual nature that will ultimately do them in. Jealousy energizes Yaldabaoth's plan for his own creation. He will make it appear just like the original divine creation, in the same indestructible pattern, creating a counterfeit. Of course, he never really saw the divine original, since his mother had banished him, but he has inherited some of his mother's power.

CHAPTER 14

Teacher/Lord/Savior/Jesus: Yaldabaoth's ego swells up when he sees his whole creation and the multitude of Yaldabaoth-designed angels/demons surrounding him.

Yaldabaoth (Chief Demon/Ruler): Listen, I tell you. I'm a jealous God, and no other god exists besides me!

Teacher/Lord/Savior/Jesus: But the fanfare exposes his vanity and falsity. If there really were no other god, then what's he jealous about?

Meanwhile, as Yaldabaoth demonstrates the darkness and absurdity of a self-made god, the mother (Sophia) begins to come to terms with the problem. She starts moving back and forth between the realm of perfect goodness and the depth of the darkness that has no foundation. Through her wisdom, she realizes the deficiency. The brightness of her God-bestowed light is fading because her partner had not been with her when she conceived the idea of an offspring.

John, the disciple: But, Lord, what do you mean that she was moving back and forth?

Teacher/Lord/Savior/Jesus: You amuse me, John. Let me explain.

Don't confuse Sophia's movement with Moses's description of the creation of the world when he said there was movement upon the waters. When God originally swept over the face of the waters, God also announced the presence of light that separated light from darkness.

But the difference with the movement of Sophia is that when the extent of the evil that came from her offspring dawns on her, she becomes horrified. In contrast with the generous actions of the Invisible Spirit, Yaldabaoth had stolen the light.

Correction by Repentance

Teacher/Lord/Savior/Jesus: Stunned with the implications of this evil act, Sophia repents.

Wisdom (*Sophia*) is in the perfect place to enact the right response to all the evil unleashed by Yaldabaoth. In repentance, she faces the darkness squarely. She can discern the utter forgetfulness of her right place in the heavenly kingdom. This ignorance darkens all the glory she had known before.

Knowing she has to face the shame, she dares not return, and this is why she vacillates back and forth. She belongs to the family of God, but her actions did not. The generation of those inhabiting the divine community practices stillness—that is, no agitation, no pull between two powers.

But wisdom distinguishes the difference. This arrogant power-grabber had taken power from his mother. She recognizes his ignorance for what it is: he has no knowledge of the realm he came from. He had known only what his mother allowed for him, so he exalted himself over his own creation of the multitude of demons/angels.

In contrast with the heavenly glorification of the One, the mother understands the miscarriage of this overblown ego and that her partner had not been in harmony with her when she conceived the idea.

Her repentance runs deep, generating inconsolable weeping. But her regret is sincere, and her community hears her entreaty. Her acknowledgment of the mistake, her turn from it, and her fervent desire to reunite with the original goodness brings forth the greatest beauty of the pristine and perfect Spirit. The whole community, dwelling in the fullness of good, rises to support the one who had been missing.

As always, they praise the source of infinite goodness, the Invisible Spirit, and now they praise this constancy of good on behalf of Sophia. In response, He pours out the abundance of Spirit upon her. Through this fullness, her partner comes to her, ready to fill in the deficiency that had caused such harm. This loving act encourages Sophia to keep moving in the right direction.

Even though she is not ready to fully embrace the meaning of her restoration, she has all the support she needs until the deficiency is fully met.

CHAPTER 15

Teacher/Lord/Savior/Jesus: Suddenly a voice becomes audible. It does not occur in mortal time, but in consciousness, because it comes from the highest realms.

The Creator God: The perfect Human exists!

Teacher/Lord/Savior/Jesus: Yaldabaoth had not known it, but the perfect Human and the Child of the perfect Human existed before he (Yaldabaoth, the Chief Ruler) could hear the news. All he knows of that realm is his mother, so he wrongly assumes that this voice was from her. The only true source of the voice—the holy Mother-Father, the complete and perfect Forethought, the image of the invisible—is inconceivable to him. In fact, the true Father of everything, in whom everything came to be, exposes the empty, fraudulent claims of Yaldabaoth.

To him, this first Human appears as a portrait statue. And yet the mere hint of the existence of the true Human is enough for all of Yaldabaoth's realm to quake. The deepest foundations of the abyss have been moved. From Yaldabaoth's perspective, the place where his mother dwelled was above the waters that covered the sky. This perfect Human, whose appearance was announced, comes from the light, causing the presence of the Human to illumine the waters above the material realm of Yaldabaoth.

The image of this first Human appears as a reflection in the water. All the demons and Chief Ruler gazed up at this spectacle toward the underside of the heavenly shining waters. And through this light, they see the image upon the waters.

Creation from a Fit of Jealousy

Teacher/Lord/Savior/Jesus: In a fit of jealousy, Yaldabaoth coaxes his subordinate demons.

Yaldabaoth (Chief Demon/Chief Ruler): Come on, let's create a human according to the image of God, but in *our* likeness! This way, the light from the image will illuminate *us*.

Teacher/Lord/Savior/Jesus: So in full compliance with his will, the demons/ angels begin to create. Using each other's powers, according to the characteristics given to them, all the demons collaborate on creating a human being. Each demonic authority contributes to the human's psyche some characteristic corresponding to the model of the image. The psyche, sometimes called soul, is the in-between place between the naturally inanimate powers of the demons and the invisible Spirit. A person might be inclined either toward the image of God or toward the likeness of the demons at any time.

Quite proud of their created being, Yaldabaoth and his minions agree to call him Adam, hoping that his name could become a power of light they still lacked. The construction of the human psyche through the acts of the seven powers begins.

Goodness creates the bone-psyche.

Forethought creates the connecting tissue for the psyche.

Divinity makes the flesh-psyche.

Lordship makes the marrow for the psyche.

Kingdom creates the blood-psyche.

Zeal creates the skin-psyche.

And intelligence makes the hair-psyche.

All the demons and authorities gather around and take these seven substances of the psyche (soul) from the powers, so that they can create the body with limbs. They put all the body parts together and coordinate them.

CHAPTER 16

Teacher/Lord/Savior/Jesus: Each demon appointed to a particular body part is named.[2] For instance, the first one, Raphaō, begins by making the head, Abron creates the skull, and so forth. One demon is responsible for each of the following body parts: the brain, the right eye, the left eye, the right ear, the left ear, the nose, the lips, the front teeth, the tonsils, the uvula, the back of the neck, the neck bone, the throat, the right shoulder, the left shoulder, the right elbow, the left elbow, the palm of the right hand, the palm of the left hand, the back of the right hand, the back of the left hand, the fingers of the right hand, the fingers of the left hand, the right nipple, the left nipple, the right armpit, the left armpit, the bodily cavity, the navel, the abdomen, the right side, the left side, the lower back on the right, the lower back on the left, the marrow, the skeleton, the stomach, the heart, the lungs, the liver, the spleen, the intestines, the kidneys, the connective tissue (or nervous

---

2. The names of all the demons associated with the construction of the body—often called angels in antiquity—are unknown to modern readers. They are not listed in this paraphrase, because their names are meaningless now. However, the list of the corresponding demons and body parts is available in Appendix A. Knowing the names of demons was a critical source of power for healers, because calling a demon by name gave would-be healers authority over the demon and thus the capacity to cast it out.

system), the vertebrae, the veins, the arteries, the pneumatic system within all the limbs, all the flesh, the right buttock, the left buttock, the penis, the testicles, the private parts, the right thigh, the left thigh, the muscles of the right thigh, the muscles of the left thigh, the right knee, the left knee, the right leg, the left leg, the right ankle, the left ankle, the right foot, the toes of the right foot, the left foot, the toes of the left foot, and the toenails.

The same seven powers (listed in chapter 12) are ordained and in charge of this elaborate construction.

CHAPTER 17

Teacher/Lord/Savior/Jesus:
Each demon who provides activation in the limbs is also named.[3] The activated body parts include the head, the back of the neck, the right shoulder, the left shoulder, the right hand, the left hand, the fingers of the right hand, and the fingers of the left hand, the right nipple, the left nipple, the chest, the right armpit, the left armpit, the right side, the left side, the bodily cavity, the abdomen, the right thigh, the left thigh, all the private parts, the right knee, the left knee, the left leg, the right leg, the right ankle, the left ankle, the right foot, the toes of the right foot, the left foot, the toes of the left foot.

And the seven powers in charge of this activation process are also listed.

Then other human characteristics are produced by similarly identified demonic powers—perception, reception, imagination, integration, and impulse.

The four *sources* of bodily demons are heat, cold, wetness, and dryness, and their mother is matter. She mixes with them and nourishes them.

Above all these worker-demons are the four chief demons, who are associated with pleasure, desire, grief, and fear. Each of these working demons is named, and they are also mothered by another demon. She enables them to produce the four terrifying passions: grief, pleasure, desire, and fear. Humans need to stay most alert to these passions, because they manipulate mind and body. Here is what each one can cause:

---

3. Again, these demons are not listed by name in this paraphrase, because their names are meaningless now. But the list of the corresponding demons and body parts they activate is available in Appendix A.

- Grief can cause envy, jealousy, suffering, distress, heartlessness, anxiety, mourning, and so forth.

- Pleasure can cause an abundance of evil and unmerited pride.

- Desire can cause anger, fury, bitterness, bitter yearning, and insatiable greed.

- Fear can cause terror, flattery, suffering, and shame.

In a confusing way for humans, these passions can appear as a mixture of virtues and vices. The head of the material *psyche* ("soul") discerns the true character of these passions.

In summary, there are 365 angels/demons (or, messengers) who labor with each part of the human creature until the psychic and material aspects are completed.

Narrator: The Redeemer, who has been explaining the identity of the demons/angels and their specific assignments, pauses to mention that there are even more demons that rule over other body parts. If you want to know about them, he tells us that we can find them in the book of Zoroaster. And he resumes his story.

CHAPTER 18

Teacher/Lord/Savior/Jesus: But then, after the work of the demons is completed, they wait. . . . And nothing happens. Their product, the psychic body, lies still for a very long time.

The Saving Begins

Teacher/Lord/Savior/Jesus: Meanwhile, Yaldabaoth's mother, Sophia, seizes the opportunity. She is eager to take back the power she had turned over to the Chief Ruler (Yaldabaoth), and she (Wisdom) has the perfect characteristics to see the danger of this mixture of light and material darkness—and also the source of its remedy. She tries to restore her proper original relationship to the Mother-Father by earnestly asking for help.

With abundant mercy, the Mother-Father takes action to help Sophia and sends down the five lights with a plan. The five lights appear in a form that appeals to Yaldabaoth. They look like wise advisers to Yaldabaoth, and they trick him into relinquishing the power of his mother.

Five Lights (representing the Mother-Father): Breathe into the face of this inanimate body by your spirit, Yaldabaoth, and that will cause this human body to rise up.

Teacher/Lord/Savior/Jesus: Because of Yaldabaoth's innate ignorance, he does not realize that by doing so, he will relinquish the Spirit-power of his mother. But, eager to become a god of mortals, he blows his spirit into the face of the psychic body. Wisdom knows, though, that her power will abandon Yaldabaoth and dwell in the psychic body that the demons had created in their likeness, but in the image of the original.

Narrator: As an aside, the work of the demons/angels begins to merge with the goals and powers of the rulers/authorities. So now the demons and rulers also become interchangeable.

Teacher/Lord/Savior/Jesus: True enough. Wisdom got it right. Now the body moves! It grows powerful, and it shines with the light from the invisible Spirit.

To his horror, Yaldabaoth and all his fellow powers/rulers realize what has happened, and they become enraged with jealousy. They had united their efforts to bring the human into being, had given him their power, and now his understanding is far greater than theirs! Even greater than the understanding of the Chief Demon (Yaldabaoth). It occurs to them that their human is luminous with the light from above, he can think better than they can, and he is completely stripped of evil. In their rage, they pick him up and throw him down into the lowest part of the whole material realm.

But the blessed Mother-Father, who had encouraged Yaldabaoth to breathe his spirit into the human, also has compassion on the human being. She/He acts quickly to prevent Yaldabaoth's demons/rulers from overpowering the psychical body again and sends a helper from the beneficent Spirit directly to Adam. Once again, a form of light is sent to the rescue.

A light-filled Insight—called Life—appears to Adam. She is always present to help the entire creation. Now She is ready to work with Adam and to restore him to his rightful relationship with the continuity of good. Also known as the Life of light, She teaches Adam how the psyche aspect of life has come to be.

Insight/Life: Wisdom has caused the seed of light to descend to the lowest parts of the mortal realm. And in the mixture with the darkness, Wisdom (Sophia) is able to reveal the return path upward.

Teacher/Lord/Savior/Jesus: This light-filled Insight hides in Adam, where the demons/rulers cannot detect it. But it remains safely with the human as a corrective to any form of deficiency that would cut humans off from the light.

CHAPTER 19

Teacher/Lord/Savior/Jesus: Even within the darkest part of the material realm, the shadow of the light within Adam makes him visible to the demons/rulers—those who had tried to create him in their likeness. Everything about his mentality is simply superior to all of them, and they know it. They have to look up to see him, and they can't avoid this stark realization.

The Battle over Mind and Body

Teacher/Lord/Savior/Jesus: All the rulers/demons now plot together to bring him at least into the shadow of death, to make him mortal. They mix fire, earth, and water with four blazing winds to cause a great turmoil. Here they enclose their human, so they can remake him fully under their control in matter.

This time the rulers/demons use more earth, water, and wind. An additional spirit of matter induces ignorance, darkness, insatiable desire, and a counterfeit spirit with no truth in it. Matter causes them to think and act like mortals who forget their true spiritual identity and heritage. The new kind of body prepared for the mortal human has become a virtual tomb! These criminal rulers/powers/authorities clothe their mortal in this body and chain him to it with the power of forgetfulness.

Demons/Rulers: If he could just forget the light of his origin, this poor mortal will remain under the control of Yaldabaoth's powers.

Teacher/Lord/Savior/Jesus: Now you know how Adam becomes a mortal person, the first to descend from the light, and the first to become estranged.

But, that light! The light that had hidden inside Adam remains hidden within, where the demonic powers cannot detect it. It continues to work for Adam and will awaken his thinking.

CHAPTER 20

Teacher/Lord/Savior/Jesus: The rulers/authorities believe they can keep him under their control by taking him to paradise.

Demons/Rulers: Look around, Adam! Look at whatever looks good.

Teacher/Lord/Savior/Jesus: In fact, though, the rulers'/authorities' pleasure is abusive, and the beauty of their gift is perverse. The pleasure they offer is a trap, and the very trees are seductive. The fruit on them is poisonous, and they promise death. And in the middle of paradise, they place their own tree of life.

Narrator: John's teacher pauses here to point out what's going on in the garden.

Teacher/Lord/Savior/Jesus: I will teach you—John and your friends—the secret of the false rulers'/authorities' lives and what they're all about. This way you'll see from the outside what Adam is facing in the midst of his dream.

The root of this tree in the middle of the garden is bitter and produces branches that cause death. You can see the hatred in the shadow under the tree, and the leaves above are designed to entrap. Its cycle of life is the pattern of mortality. Look at the blossoms that come from darkness and produce the ointment of evil. The fruit kills, and the seed produces a false desire for more. Whoever ingests this fruit lives in perpetual torment, the place of everlasting darkness.

However, there is another tree in the garden, the one they call the tree of the knowledge of good and evil. The rulers/authorities/powers know it as the source of true intelligence, the light that would rescue anyone from darkness. So, they try to block Adam's view of it. They're aware that if this mortal caught a glimpse of it, he would recognize its fullness and then become more conscious of his own condition of shame.

But you need to realize, John, that I'm the one who encouraged the human to go ahead and eat of this tree!

John, the disciple: And I was rather startled to hear this, because what I learned in Genesis is that the snake is the one who taught Adam to eat from the tree that would cause his downfall.

Teacher/Lord/Savior/Jesus: Ah, I know, John. The snake had an evil intent. *My* intent was to awaken Adam. But consider how the snake tried to create false desires in Adam. If he could do that, the snake would be able to seduce him after he gained the knowledge from the tree, and then he (Adam) would ultimately be a servant to the snake.

But the truth is, the snake knew all along that Adam would resist it. The light actually dwells in Adam, and his thinking is more correct than the distorted thinking of the Chief Ruler/Chief Demon. This is why I encouraged him to take hold of the light from the tree. He was going to need to correct the thinking imposed on him by the rulers/demons.

CHAPTER 21

Teacher/Lord/Savior/Jesus: Let me explain a little more. The snake can't really seduce Adam, so he hypnotizes him. He causes him to fall into a deep sleep, in order to manipulate his mind. Yaldabaoth takes over, making Adam completely forgetful of who he is, where he comes from, and the fact that he possesses the light and power from above. His aim was to recapture the power that he had blown into Adam's face when he first tried to animate him.

John, the disciple: But I want to know about this trance, and I ask the Savior directly, "What does it mean to be in a deep sleep?"

Teacher/Lord/Savior/Jesus: Well, it's not quite as simple as you heard about it from Genesis, when a deep sleep fell on Adam, and a rib was taken from him by which the woman was created. It's more like what the prophet Isaiah heard during a time of national crisis:

Isaiah: Make the mind of this people dull, and stop their ears, and shut their eyes, so that they may not look with their eyes, and listen with their ears, and comprehend with their minds, and turn and be healed (Isaiah 6:10 NRSV).

Teacher/Lord/Savior/Jesus: The Israelites had turned from their God and were no longer able to perceive the divine guidance. Their prophet Isaiah warned that their hearts would be heavy, and their minds would become dull just when they needed God's help.

Adam and Eve, Victims Saved

Teacher/Lord/Savior/Jesus: This was the type of involuntary and mesmeric trance that Yaldabaoth caused in Adam.

But, despite the vicious attack on Adam's capacity to even think his own thoughts, the light-filled insight remains hidden within him. The Chief Ruler/Yaldabaoth knows it is still there, so while Adam is still under the control of his hypnotic spell, he attempts to remove the light from Adam's rib cage.

It is impossible to grasp the insight of light, however, either physically or mentally. Even though darkness pursues it, Yaldabaoth fails to take hold of the light.

He does, however, succeed in taking some portion of his power back from Adam that he (Yaldabaoth) needs to create a person with a woman's form. Using this power, he creates another being, modeled after the Insight of light, still within Adam. He places this power into the molded form of womanhood. This was not the rib from the account of creation in Genesis.

But suddenly, Adam can see this woman beside him. At that moment, the Insight is lit, becomes visible, and lifts the veil from Adam's dulled mind. It is as if he becomes sober after a drunken state of darkness, and within moments, he recognizes his likeness in her, from the light.

Adam: We are of the same flesh and bones! And this is why men should leave their fleshly parents and cleave to their wives. When they discover this oneness, they are no longer two, but one.

Teacher/Lord/Savior/Jesus: A partner will be sent to Adam so that the original full male-female partner arrangement in the heavenly realm is reflected in the human experience.

The wisdom of Wisdom (*Sophia*) has come to full fruition, because the deficiency of her wholeness has been corrected. When evil spews forth and attempts to (re-)create humanity in the likeness of a false, arrogant ego, its ignorance is exposed. Its evil motives are overcome by the light that never self-extinguishes.

Wisdom, our true sister, descends to the greatest danger, where humanity might have forgotten their divine rights and legitimacy. When she does this, we know her also as Life (*Zoe*), the mother of the living. She meets this terrible, threatening enemy squarely and speaks with absolute authority so that no one is deprived of the fullness of life. It is through her wisdom that all humanity is aware of all they need to know in the face of the wiles and tactics of the enemy.

Yaldabaoth and his fellow demons/rulers have not yet resorted to every form of ammunition.

Wisdom/Sophia: But I have come to comfort my people with the assurance of my final authority.

Teacher/Lord/Savior/Jesus: I also have come to protect against the onslaught of the enemy. I come to accompany the Insight of light, and together we take on the appearance of an eagle (myself) on the special tree (the tree of knowledge).

Both Adam and Eve become enclosed in a mortal corpse, but the knowledge from the tree informs them of their state of shame and nakedness. I come to awaken them from the depth of this mesmerizing sleep, so that I can teach them what they need to know. The Insight of light also appears to them to rouse their thought.

CHAPTER 22

Teacher/Lord/Savior/Jesus: Before long, they find their way outside of Yaldabaoth's imprisoning camp. But as soon as Yaldabaoth knows they have withdrawn from him, he curses his earth. Immediately setting off to find them, he discovers Eve preparing herself for Adam. Unaware of the holy design of egalitarian relationships, Yaldabaoth gives her over to Adam, so that he will be her master.

Yaldabaoth exposes his ignorance of the divine order by misusing his power. His concept of power involves exerting it over others to imprison them. But this abuse of power draws attention to its exact opposite, the Invisible Spirit. True power is known by its *empowering* of good in others throughout the whole realm.

Adam and Eve are still under the spell of Yaldabaoth's demonic powers, so they're too frightened to rebuke him. The demons have no trouble recognizing the Chief Demon's arrogance and empty ignorance, but they act under orders. Adam and Eve are expelled from the garden, and Yaldabaoth dresses them in dark gloom.

But Yaldabaoth's quest for power is insatiable, and he can't leave them alone either. He finds the virgin, Eve, once again, standing with her husband. There she is, with the light-filled Insight radiating through her, and any sense of good completely evaporates from Yaldabaoth.

Mortal Life in Matter

Teacher/Lord/Savior/Jesus: Immediately, the Forethought of the true realm can sense what is about to happen. She sends some clear thoughts for Eve, assuring her that Life (*Zoe*) was not inside her body. Then Yaldabaoth rapes her. Even in the intensity of this vile act, Eve herself is protected. Her life is not in the body, so he cannot take it. He only mates with the fleshly creation of his own doing, thereby perpetuating his own discord.

He fathers two sons from this shadow of Eve: Elohim and Yahweh. These god-sons battle over righteousness and unrighteousness with their own weapons. Yahweh holds the power of fire and wind, and Elohim controls water and earth. Ultimately Yaldabaoth renames them Cain and Abel, because they are unable to carry on the divine lineage of the holy One. Their ignorance and the limitations of matter cannot accommodate the pure image and likeness of the Invisible Spirit.

Yaldabaoth establishes the foundations of his counterfeit realm on his attempted rape of Eve. From this cruel act, intercourse becomes the jest of the demons, causing all women in his kingdom to feel manipulated by an insatiable desire, to feel dependent on men, and to simply produce babies. Worst of all, he breathes his own counterfeit spirit of life into helpless infants, perpetuating their deficiencies, and he covers up all of his deeds with a deceptive appearance of the real Spirit of Life. To seal off the fate of this generation of people, Yaldabaoth commands Elohim (Cain) and Yahweh (Abel) to keep guard over all of them to be certain everyone will die. One preserves the certainty of death for the body, and the other, the certainty of death for the earth.

The Psyche Life of Matter and Spirit Combined

Teacher/Lord/Savior/Jesus: On the other hand, another type of creation is also taking place. The first is a counterfeit tale of the true story. These are not two creations, but alternate views of creation. In the second case, Adam perceives the likeness of his own prior self-understanding, and the offspring appears from this conscious awareness. No intercourse is required, but Adam begets a son like the Child of the true Human. Adam names him Seth and acknowledges that he has appeared in the same way the generations appear in the heavenly realm of the Invisible Spirit.

The Mother (Wisdom), who bestows the life-giving Spirit, also participates in Seth's completeness. She extends the female elements through the fullness of the Spirit so that all succeeding descendants will have access to full support.

However, in this second account of creation, the Chief Ruler still has the capacity to mess with the minds of the humans. So, his line of attack is to force the humans to drink from the waters of forgetfulness. If they would just forget who they were and where they had come from, Yaldabaoth could continue to manipulate them.

Just as Sophia had been temporarily cut off from her full participation in the heavenly realm due to her participation in a supposed life apart from the One, so the children of Seth are temporarily rendered subservient to the Chief Ruler.

And yet, the Spirit will return to correct their off-course drift away from their roots. Their deficiency in this knowledge will be restored and fully healed. Spirit will not fail, because it is impossible for a deficiency to exist in the heavenly realm. It is holy and fully populated by those who praise the One.

John's Deepest Questions

CHAPTER 23

John, the disciple: Learning the full story of creation and how evil is such a fraudulent deception, I (John) can't help but wonder whether and how everyone is to be saved from these evil forces. I ask more questions.

My first question: Lord, will everyone be led safely to this pure light you speak of?

Before I get a straight answer, the Savior compliments me on my being receptive to his teaching. He says it's difficult to explain these things to those who don't recognize their true origin in the realm of those who simply do not waver.

Then he tells me plainly that:

Teacher/Lord/Savior/Jesus: the Spirit of Life is what saves. When this Spirit reaches people with its power to bless, they realize their perfection and their worthiness of great good. Spirit will protect them from demonic passions and evil forces. The pure light keeps them on the path to the truly enduring good, protecting them from fleshly temptations that ultimately lead to failure—anger, envy, jealousy, false desire, or greed.

John, the disciple: I am concerned, though. *My second question*: But, what about those who still feel angry, jealous, and greedy after the Spirit of Life came to them? Will they make it?

Teacher/Lord/Savior/Jesus: I have complete confidence in the power of the transforming and saving Spirit. If the Spirit comes to them, they will be saved. This power will descend on every single human being. In fact, no one can even stand up without it. Remember how Adam had all the features of the human body but could not even move until the breath of Spirit was blown into him? This is the same Spirit that comes when a child is born.

When Spirit comes to strengthen each individual, that one is incapable of being led astray into wickedness. The difficulty lies in the way the counterfeit spirit works. If someone is seduced by that false spirit, they can be led astray until they reconnect with the true Spirit that was there in the first place.

John, the disciple: The Savior doesn't fully answer my question about whether everyone will be led safely yet. But I expect he will return to this after I ask another pressing question.

My third question: Lord, what happens to those who transition out of their flesh? Where do they go?

First he laughs. Maybe he thinks it's so obvious that the soul is strong and has more power than the wicked counterfeit spirit.

Teacher/Lord/Savior/Jesus: When the Spirit has strengthened them, they do not need the flesh in order to flee the evil. Rather, the power they obtain from the pure Spirit will not become weak and corruptible. It safely guides them to their permanent, undisturbed peace.

John, the disciple: Then I want to ask about the people who succumb to the false attractions of the counterfeit spirit.

My fourth question: Lord, what about those who don't even know who they belong to? What if their forgetfulness prevents them from even trying to follow the light?

Teacher/Lord/Savior/Jesus: Sadly, this is what happens when the contemptible counterfeit spirit has grown stronger and leads them astray. They end up doing the works of wickedness, and their souls are burdened. The false authorities take over, manipulate them, bind them with powers of their own, and imprison them in their own bodies.

It just stays this way until they awaken, and they gain awareness of the continuity of good. Not death, but the knowledge of this good, is what they need to be corrected and saved.

John, the disciple: Now I want to know how it happens.

My fifth question: How do we actually get back to that original perfection? Does the soul just shrink down to the nature of its mother or the human?

The Lord is happy with this question, because he says it is evident that I understand. I do understand that we're not being asked to shrink back into our mother's womb to restart our lives or expect a kind of reincarnation. But by going forward and discovering the Spirit of Life, we are saved from the passions that speak to us through the flesh.

I'm happy to realize that everybody has a chance to be saved from the deceptive powers of demons. But I'm still concerned.

My sixth question: Lord, what about those who have gained the true gnosis (knowledge of the continuity of good) and *still* turn away voluntarily? What happens to them?

Teacher/Lord/Savior/Jesus: Well, it's not good for the people who intentionally disobey. They are the ones bringing eternal punishment on themselves. There is no judge waiting at the door. They'll be admitted by their own decision not to repent. They may *think* they want to rebel and live according to their own arrogance, but they are creating their own eternal punishment.

John, the disciple: This is why my first question was wondering if *everyone* would ultimately be saved. Since the Lord had already told me that the power of Spirit would come to every single human being, I now understand that the punishment is eternal for those who do not bring themselves to repent.

CHAPTER 24

John, the disciple: I'm grateful to understand now how everyone will be led safely to the pure light. But one more question presses on me.

My bonus question: Lord, where did the evil, counterfeit spirit come from?

He looks at me with such tenderness and replies,

Teacher/Lord/Savior/Jesus: you know that the one truth, the one reality, is the Mother-Father who loves you.

The Savior Explains How People Became Duped by Evil

Narrator: Now the Teacher/Lord/Savior/Jesus retells the story of the way we were deluded by the counterfeit spirit.

Teacher/Lord/Savior/Jesus: Here is what happened. Let me explain another way. Everything began with the Mother-Father who is holy in every way and compassionately cares for you (and everyone). The light-giving Forethought awakened the thinking of the perfect generation. But the Chief Ruler knew all too well that your whole Human generation surpassed him with your excellent intelligence. In his fury, he and his fellow authorities, in committing adultery with Sophia, forced pollution onto the goodness of the land. Everyone knows that adultery blurs the lines separating one family from another, so the evil intent was to undermine the structure of the entire creation.

They planned to beget bitter Fate through her, and fate is as unpredictable and cruel as any demon. It is stronger than the gods, authorities, demons, and people who are caught up in it. Sinfulness, violence, selfishness, ignorance, fear, and blinding ignorance take over the minds of its victims. Fate would have maintained complete mastery over the people, but the despicable counterfeit spirit had not yet conquered the human.

Yaldabaoth needs a new plan. He regrets all that he brought into being, and he is determined now to flood out the entire human population.

Narrator: Readers of the Bible will recognize the story of the Yaldabaoth's desire to destroy the whole creation resembles the story of the flood encountered by Noah in the book of Genesis.

Teacher/Lord/Savior/Jesus: Despite Yaldabaoth's dark plan, Noah discerns the light of Insight that is always present in the midst of the darkest forms of opposition. He learned from this light what to do to protect at least those who would listen to him. He warns everyone, and only the skeptics ignore him.

Narrator: Again, this account is a bit different from the way Moses told the story, or whoever it was who actually wrote it in the book of Genesis.

Teacher/Lord/Savior/Jesus: Many of the people from the realm of pure stillness join Noah in a cloud of light. Ironically, it is the luminous cloud that hides them from the all-consuming darkness of the flood. From this source of light, Noah knows his authority. He has been empowered by the One source of light, and everyone who chose to enter into it with Noah is protected.

CHAPTER 25

Teacher/Lord/Savior/Jesus: But since the flood failed to destroy humankind, Yaldabaoth works on another plan with his co-powers. He sends them to human women, so that they can father their own children through the women, entirely for the sake of their own pleasures.

That plan was a flop. Women were not that foolish.

So, in his fury, Yaldabaoth polishes his counterfeit likeness to create a despicable spirit resembling the true Spirit as perfectly as possible. The demons/powers then present themselves to the women again, only this time appearing in the images of their spouses. Their goal is the same—to rape them and to pollute their souls.

The demons/powers bring beautiful gifts and everything the women could imagine wanting. Then, having seduced them, these false demons/powers gradually mix darkness and wickedness into their everyday lives. By now, the counterfeit powers/gods appear to have won. Desire has taken control of the minds of both women and men, and it leads them into the ways of error.

People grow old with no enjoyment, and they die without finding any truth or even knowing the true God. Demons/powers continue to take the women and cause them to bear children out of darkness in the likeness of those powers. The hearts of all the people become closed and hardened by the despicable spirit.

This is the sad tale of how the whole world has become enslaved.

The Savior Forethought Tells her Story

CHAPTER 26

Narrator: But now the perfect Forethought appears again. She tells the rest of the story in her own words:

Perfect Forethought/Savior: I have taken on the appearance of my offspring, so they might discern the difference between the seductive spirits and me. I have been here for them all along, never abandoning my children. I continue to produce the abundance of light they need, and I cause them to have what they most need: the memory of who they really are.

I need to find them where they are. I persevere until I find them and discover they have been kept prisoner by their own confusion and vast darkness. My very presence shakes the foundations of this earthly dream. So forcefully I disturb the evil powers, that even I know I need to hide from the people I have come to rescue.

I come back for a second time, conscious that I come from the source of light and that I bring the memory so essential to the escape. I enter the midst of the darkness, right into the heart of hell itself and with the conviction of my authority to reestablish the law and order of life. This time, the foundations of this cruel prison are shaken with such violence, it appears these very foundations will collapse upon those who dwell in the chaos. I flee again to my home in the light to spare the people from being destroyed in the attack on the prison.

When I return for the third time, I repeat the journey. First, I establish again that I am grounded in the light and full memory of our origins in the good. Then I travel to the midst of the darkness, back into the heart of hell. I am prepared to allow the fullness of my light to reveal who I am and my purpose in being there.

Arriving in the deepest confines of the prison, where their minds and bodies are heavily shackled, I call out, "Whoever can hear me, wake up from this deep sleep!" Someone starts to stir. I can hear the weeping and shedding of heavy tears. After gaining composure, a voice emerges from the dark shadows,

Prisoner: Who is calling my name?! And where is my hope coming from as I lie in the fetters of this prison?

Perfect Forethought/Savior: I answer you with a heart full of compassion. I am the Forethought from the heavenly realm, and I have been sent by the pure and divine Spirit to help you and to bring you home. First, I am ready to raise you up, so you can realize how honored you really are. Now *you* are ready to rise up with the strength of Spirit, because you can remember what you have heard! Be wise now, and follow your inner light. This is your own root, leading you directly to me—the source of compassion.

You know enough now to be on your guard against the demonic influences that steal your joy and your innocence. Take care and reject the seductive demons who try to deceive and confuse you. Pay special attention to the temptation to merely seek comfort. It puts you to sleep right when you need to be awake! You can detect that dream that draws you unwittingly right into the depths of Hades. You have all that you need to make this escape, because, in my compassion, I have brought you everything.

As with everyone who calls for help, I raised you up and washed you with the baptismal light of the water. Death will no longer hold any power over you.

John Recaps His Revelation: The Story of Healing and Restoration

CHAPTER 27

Narrator: And now the healing messenger has finished responding to the call for help.

John, the disciple: We have been told everything so that we can give to anyone else who is willing to hear. It will appear as a secret to those who close their ears. The promise of unshakable peace is a mystery for those who will not look more deeply.

We treasure this awakening and commit to preserving it for all humanity. We would be cursed to the depths of our being if we exchanged this gift from God for any type of earthly pleasures and glory. These things come in the purity of heart-to-heart prayer with God. And then the presence leaves us, so that we can go out to share it freely with anyone willing to hear.

Jesus Christ Amen!

Narrator: This is the secret revelation according to John.

APPENDIX A

Demons and Their Powers over the Body

This detailed list of the correspondence between the distinct creating powers and the body parts assigned to them exists in the longer, but not the shorter, version of the Secret Revelation of John. Scholars have not determined the reason for the discrepancy. The shorter version could be evidence of later scribes intentionally removing it. Or the longer version could include an additional section to emphasize the importance of healing various bodily ailments through these named controlling powers.

Here is the creation of Adam:

And the powers began.

The first, kindness, made an animate element of bone.

The second, forethought, made an animate element of connective tissue.

The third, divinity, made an animate element of flesh.

The fourth, lordship, made an animate element of marrow.

The fifth, kingship, made an animate element of blood.

The sixth, zeal, made an animate element of skin.

The seventh, intelligence, made an animate element of hair.

And the multitude of angels stood before him. And the seven substances of the animate subsistence[1] were taken by the authorities, so that the

---

1. Or, "soul."

regularizing of limbs and parts and the joining, i.e. ordering, of each of the constituents might be brought about.

The first, Raphaō, began by making the crown of the head;

Abrōn made the skull;

Mēniggesstrōēth made the brain;

Asterekhmē, the right eye;

Thaspomakha, the left eye;

Ierōnumos, the right ear;

Bissoum, the left ear;

Akiōreim, the nose;

Banēnephroum, the lips;

Amēn, the front teeth;

Basiliadēmē, the tonsils;

Akhkha, the uvula;

Adaban, the back of the neck;

Khaaman, the neck bone;

Dearkhō, the throat;

Tēbar, the right shoulder;

[. . .], the left shoulder;

Mniarkhōn, the right elbow;

[. . .], the left elbow;

Abitriōn, the palm of the right hand;

Euanthēn, the palm of the left hand;

Krus, the back of the right hand;

Bēluai, the back of the left hand;

Trēneu, the fingers of the right hand;

Balbēl, the fingers of the left hand;

Astrōps, the right nipple;

Barrōph, the left nipple;

Baoum, the right armpit;

Ararim, the left armpit;

Arekh, the bodily cavity;

Phthauē, the navel;

Sēnaphim, the abdomen;

Arakhethōpi, the right side;

Zabedō, the left side;

Barias, the lower back on the right;

Phnouth, the lower back on the left;

Abēnlenarkhei, the marrow;

Khnoumeninorin, the skeleton;

Gēsole, the stomach;

Agromauma, the heart;

Banō, the lungs;

Sōstrapal, the liver;

Anēsimalar, the spleen;

Thōpithrō, the intestines;

Biblō, the kidneys;

Roerōr, the connective tissue (nervous system);

Taphreō, the vertebrae;

Ipouspobōba, the veins;

Bineborin, the arteries;

Latoimenpsēphei, the pneumatic system within all the limbs;

Ēnthollei, all the flesh;

Bedouk, the right buttock;

Arabēei, the left buttock;

[. . .], the penis;

Eilō, the testicles;

Sōrma, the private parts;

Gormakaiokhlabar, the right thigh;

Nebrith, the left thigh;

Psērēm, the muscles of the right thigh;

Asaklas, the muscle of the left thigh;

Ormaōth, the right knee;

Ēmēnun, the left knee;

Knuks, the right leg;

Tupēlon, the left leg;

Akhiēl, the right ankle;

Phnēmē, the left ankle;

Phiouthrom, the right foot;

Boabel, the toes of the right foot;

Trakkhoun, the left foot;

Phikna, the toes of the left foot;

Miamai, the toenails;

Labērnium, the [. . .]

Now, those which are ordained in charge of the preceding are seven in number: Athōth; Armas; Kalila; Iabēl; Sabaōth; Cain; Abel.

And those which provide activation in the limbs are, according to parts:

First the head, Diolimodraza;

The back of the neck, Iammeaks;

The right shoulder, Iakouib;

The left shoulder, Ouertōn;

The right hand, Oudidi;

The left hand, Arbao;

The fingers of the right hand, Lampnō;

The fingers of the left hand, Lēekaphar.

The right nipple, Barbar;

The left nipple, Imaē;

The chest, Pisandiaptēs;

The right armpit, Koadē;

The left armpit Odeōr;

The right side, Asphiksiks;

The left side, Snogkhouta;

The bodily cavity, Arouph;

The abdomen, Sabalō;

The right thigh, Kharkharb;

The left thigh, Khthaōn;

All the private parts, Bathinōth;

The right knee, Khouks;

The left knee, Kharkha;

The right leg, Aroēr,

The left leg, Tōekhtha;

The right ankle, Aōl;

The left ankle, Kharanēr;

The right foot, Bastan;

The toes of the right foot, Arkhentekhtha;

The left foot, Marephnounth;

The toes of the left foot, Arbrana;

And seven were ordained in charge of the preceding:

Mikhaēl;

Ouriēl;

Asmenedas;

Saphasatoēl;

Aarmouriam;

Rikhram;

Amiōrps.[2]

2. The translation of these lists is from Layton, *Gnostic Scriptures*, 39–42.

Following these lists, the author explains that "the wellspring of the demons that are in all the body is divided in four: heat, cold, wetness, dryness. And the mother of them all is matter . . . And out of the four demons came passions" (Layton, 42–43).

Questions for Pondering Alone or in Study Groups

CHAPTER 1

1. When John (in the Secret Revelation of John) went to the mountain to pray after Jesus's death, the whole world shone with a light, and within the light, a child appeared. What did you notice about that light throughout the whole book? What did it do? When was it present? How did it appear?

2. Knowing that you're involved in a very ancient text, how are you accounting for the fact that you are reading it with so many centuries of cultural differences between you and the text?

   How would you identify the differences that impact the way you read the text?

   How would you describe the similarities that impact the way you read the text?

3. What specific church teachings influence the way you read a text that is not in the Bible?

CHAPTER 2

1. Have you ever experienced a crisis of faith similar to the predicament John found himself in?

   What happened?

   Have you moved past it, or are you still experiencing it?

2. John was being pushed to grasp a greater understanding of God as infinitely good. In the process, he had to be willing to admit the limitation of his own mind. Do you balk at the idea of an infinitely good God?

   If so, what is your hesitation?

   If not, what makes you willing to accept something beyond your own senses?

3. Can you identify some elements of time that restrict your life?

   Can you identify some timeless aspects of your life?

   In what ways does the Secret Revelation of John help to mitigate the time restrictions in your life?

4. The Secret Revelation of John is based on the idea that our true origins are in perfect goodness, not sinfulness. It agrees with the first chapter of Genesis: "So God created humankind in his image, in the image of God he created them; male and female he created them. God saw everything that he had made, and indeed, it was very good" (Genesis 1:27, 31 NRSV). Problems show up later, but our origins are in goodness.

   If you balk at this, why?

   If you accept this, why?

5. The Secret Revelation of John was written during a period of severe oppression from the Roman Empire. Can you identify how the book's defense of God's goodness might have provided relief from poverty and hunger?

   Aware of some of the painful political and social powers of the second century, can you identify some ways those powers might have had the potential to yield to the common good?

Does the Secret Revelation of John imply that only some people should receive the benefits of the heavenly realm? If so, who?

Does the Secret Revelation of John imply that justice will be available before death or only after death? What examples do you find?

CHAPTER 3

1. The author of the Secret Revelation of John uses the figure of Sophia (Wisdom) to explain how evil appeared after all creation had been established as good. The argument boils down to the idea that Wisdom awakens humanity to the truth that evil is a thunderous fraud.

   If you have a different way of explaining the presence of evil in the world, describe it.

2. The story of Yaldabaoth is a mockery of the true story of creation by the Invisible Spirit. But it explains why mortals feel mortal and sinful, rather than centered in their true identity as the likeness of Spirit, the likeness of Goodness.

   Can you relate any experiences in which you discovered you had been fooled into thinking something untrue?

   What seduced you to believe it in the first place?

   What changed your mind?

3. In the second century, it was commonly understood that demons had the power to disrupt the harmony of mind and body.

   How would you identify influences on human minds and bodies today?

4. The author of the Secret Revelation of John alters the Genesis account of the first humans. Differences from Genesis that appear in the Secret Revelation of John affect (1) the conversation between Adam and the serpent, (2) how Eve comes on the scene, and (3) the story of Noah saving many more people than his own family.

   What aspects of Genesis as altered in the Secret Revelation of John do you like? Why do you like these changes?

   What aspects of Genesis as altered in the Secret Revelation of John do you not like? Why don't you like these changes?

5. Considering that the story of Yaldabaoth is a myth intended to teach valuable lessons, what value do you find in the depiction of Yaldabaoth's rape of Eve?

Does this story impact your own view of the inherent nature of women? If so, how?

Does this story say something valuable about violence and power? If so, what?

CHAPTER 4

1. Realizing that the meaning of salvation in antiquity was quite different from the way traditional churches speak of it today, which definition are you more inclined to believe?

What aspects of salvation described in the Secret Revelation of John would you want for yourself?

2. Since Descartes bequeathed to our human era a stark split between the mind world and the matter world, are you inclined to stay with it or reconsider the notion from the Secret Revelation of John that the psyche inclines toward either of two ends of a matter–spirit spectrum? What persuades you to make this choice about your own identity?

3. What is your end-game view of the world? Describe it with as much detail as you can. Compare your views with those expressed in the Secret Revelation of John.

Will everybody ultimately be saved (before or after death)?

What happens to people who did horrific things on earth?

4. The notion of our "reflecting" implies that our goodness originates—that our identities have their origin—in something outside ourselves. This implication causes us to turn around (sometimes repenting) to see ourselves as Infinite Spirit originally "gazed" us into being. Can you describe any experiences of such conscious reflecting?

Would you say your experience was more like turning or awakening—or both?

What caused you to make the change?

5. In the Savior's explanations about salvation in the Secret Revelation of John, death does not appear much of a factor in defining what salvation is. That is, questions about salvation persist after death just as they did before death. What role does death play in your own view of an everlasting relationship with God?

6. Healing is important in the Secret Revelation of John because it is the before-death evidence of the saving method taught by the Savior.

   Describe your own experiences with this kind of salvation-healing. Some examples might be a healing of anger (passion), freedom from a stress-related illness, growing conviction of your divine rights, or release from fear.

CHAPTER 5

1. How would you describe the "secret" of the Secret Revelation of John?

   By what means is it illuminated?

   In what ways does it remain a secret in the twenty-first century?

2. Part of the evident critique in the Secret Revelation of John is levied against the hierarchical powers of the Roman Empire. And yet the Secret Revelation itself maintains a type of hierarchy in its structure of the heavenly kingdom. In what ways do modern societies reject and uphold hierarchies?

   Does the Secret Revelation of John indicate how to discern the difference between good hierarchies and bad ones? How does it convey this?

3. The power struggle between Yaldabaoth and the Invisible Spirit resembles different forms of power struggles throughout the ages. In the twenty-first century, most advocates of social justice argue that any form of excessive power or omnipotence results in injustice. But the argument in favor of Spirit's omnipotence is that it uses its supremacy to *empower* anyone who seeks that source of goodness and strengthens their opposition to evil. Can you identify contemporary examples of where such empowering would be good for society?

4. In what ways does the consistency of the message of quantum physics help you rethink the mental nature of reality?

Does the message of quantum physics fit with or challenge your assumptions of cause and effect?

What are the implications of your ideas about the message quantum physics has for our age?

5. How do you intend to treat the gems of the Secret Revelation of John?

Do you feel willing to welcome your own transformation?

How would you identify your struggles with your own transformation? What's hard to let go?

Is there any kind of human possession that would interfere with your commitment to preserving these gems for the sake of humanity?

Would you accept John's challenge to "go out to share" the gems from the Secret Revelation "freely with anyone willing to hear"?

Glossary

AEON. This Greek term is used frequently in antiquity to designate an entity of space or time, such as in a realm. In some texts, including the Secret Revelation of John, an aeon can also be personified, such as Sophia (Wisdom). An aeon is an emanation from the First Principle (God).

ARCHON. This Greek term means "ruler." It was commonly used in reference to secular rulers—specifically Roman rulers. In the Secret Revelation of John and other ancient texts, the meaning extends to powerful but deeply flawed celestial beings.

BARBELŌ. She is the first emanation of God and is depicted as a supreme female principle. Sometimes she is referred to as Mother-Father or the eternal aeon. Her/His/Its role as Mother and healer and source of being is amorphous but always the force for good.

EPINOIA. She is one of the identities of the Savior, sent by the Mother Forethought to correct conceptions of the divine realm with light or reflection and to save humanity. She is frequently identified with "the light."

FORETHOUGHT (*PRONOIA*). She is a personalized figure who foresees God's plan for salvation. Her role as a savior figure is associated with the Jewish conceptualizations of Wisdom.

GNOSIS. This is a kind of knowledge that brings about a satisfying awareness of where we have come from and where we are going. God gives it to everyone, and it connotes an experience of healing and protection from demons.

NAG HAMMADI LIBRARY. This library is actually a collection of thirteen leather-bound books (codices) whose pages are made of papyrus. The books were found near a monastery near the town of Nag Hammadi, Egypt. Each book contains several separate texts, and the Secret Revelation of John appears in three of these codices—more often than any other text in the entire collection.

SALVATION. There has never been an established doctrine of salvation. In the Secret Revelation of John, it is the process of removing or becoming free from counterfeit thoughts that impede the acknowledgement of Deity-created perfection. Complete salvation is full freedom from the influence of demons and enables one to live in the joy of the divine realm.

SETH. Seth is the third son of Adam and Eve in Genesis. When the Secret Revelation of John was written, Seth was often understood as either an allegorical or a literal ancestor of humankind. The "seed of Seth" takes on the form of the divine Humanity within the human body.

SOPHIA. *Sophia* is the Greek term for wisdom and appears in a personified form in the Secret Revelation of John. She is the pivotal figure because of her divine origin, her link to the flawed creation, her repentance, and her unique ability to save those who suffer.

YALDABAOTH. He is the offspring of the flawed expression of the divine aeon, Sophia. He declares himself the Chief Ruler of his entire counterfeit creation, which is a mockery of the divine. His work is exposed as a counterfeit and is overthrown by the true God and the saviors sent to rescue humanity.

Sources Cited

Antonakou, Elena I., and Lazaros C. Triarhou. "Soul, Butterfly, Mythological Nymph: Psyche in Philosophy and Neuroscience." *Arquivos de Neuro-Psiquiatria* 75 (2017) 176–79.

Boyarin, Daniel. *Dying for God: Martyrdom and the Making of Christianity and Judaism.* Stanford: Stanford University Press, 1999.

Brooks, Michael. "Matter of Interpretation." *New Scientist: The Collection—The Quantum World* 3.3 (2016) 16–19.

———. "Spooky Action at a Distance: Entanglement." *New Scientist: The Collection—The Quantum World* 3.3 (2016) 11–13.

Davies, Stevan L., trans. *The Secret Book of John: The Gnostic Gospel Annotated and Explained.* SkyLight Illuminations. Woodstock, VT: Skylight Paths, 2005.

Dunn, James D. G. *Christology in the Making: A New Testament Inquiry into the Origins of the Doctrine of the Incarnation.* 2nd ed. London: SCM, 1989.

Eddy, Mary Baker. *Science and Health with Key to the Scriptures.* Boston: The Christian Science Publishing Society, 1934.

Eliade, Mircea. *The Myth of the Eternal Return, or Cosmos and History.* Translated by Willard R. Trask. 1954. Reprint, Bollingen Series 46. Princeton: Princeton University Press, 2005.

Elliott, Susan M. (Elli). *Family Empires, Roman and Christian.* Vol. 1, *Roman Family Empires: Household, Empire, Resistance.* 2 vols. Salem, OR: Polebridge, 2018.

Foerster, W. "Daimon." *Theological Dictionary of the New Testament,* edited by Gerhard Kittel, 2:1–20. Translated by Geoffrey W. Bromiley. 10 vols. Grand Rapids: Eerdmans, 1977.

Gaither, Carl C., and Alma E. Cavazos-Gaither, eds., *Gaither's Dictionary of Scientific Quotations: A Collection of Approximately 27,000 Quotations Pertaining to Archaeology, Architecture, Astronomy, Technology, Theory, Universe, and Zoology.* London: Springer, 2012.

Giversen, Søren. *Apocryphon Johannis: The Coptic Text of the Apocryphon Johannis in the Nag Hammadi Codex II with Translation, Introduction and Commentary.* Acta theologica Danica 5. Copenhagen: Munksgaard, 1963.

Grierson, Bruce. "What If Age Is Nothing but a Mind-Set?" *New York Times,* October 22, 2014. https://www.nytimes.com/2014/10/26/magazine/what-if-age-is-nothing-but-a-mind-set.html.

Hagerty, Barbara Bradley. *Fingerprints of God: The Search for the Science of Spirituality*. New York: Riverhead, 2009.

Harry Potter Wiki. "Albus Dumbledore." https://harrypotter.fandom.com/wiki/Albus_ Dumbledore

Heisenberg, Werner. *Physics and Philosophy: The Revolution in Modern Science*. Gifford Lectures 1955/56. World Perspectives. New York: Harper & Row, 1992.

Henry, Richard. "The Mental Universe." *Nature* 436/29 (2005).https://doi.org/10.1038/ 436029a.

The Holy Bible. New Revised Standard Version. Oxford: Oxford University, 1989.

Humble, Susan E. "Sophia the Enigma." Research Project to earn a Master's of Theological Studies from Claremont School of Theology, 2005.

Johnson-DeBaufre, Melanie. *Jesus among Her Children: Q, Eschatology, and the Construction of Christian Origins*. Harvard Theological Studies 55. Cambridge: Harvard University Press, 2005.

King, Karen L. *The Secret Revelation of John*. Cambridge: Harvard University Press, 2006.

Layton, Bentley. *The Gnostic Scriptures: Ancient Wisdom for the New Age*. Anchor Bible Reference Library. New York: Doubleday, 1987.

Lillie, Celene. *The Rape of Eve: The Transformation of Roman Ideology in Three Early Christian Retellings of Genesis*. Minneapolis: Fortress, 2017.

Meyer, Marvin, ed. *The Nag Hammadi Scriptures: The Revised and Updated Translation of Sacred Gnostic Texts*. International ed. New York: HarperOne, 2007.

Paulson, Shirley. "Healing Theologies in Christian Science and Secret Revelation of John: A Critical Conversation in Practical Theology." PhD diss., University of Birmingham, 2017.

Plotinus. *Ennead*.

Ramelli, Ilaria. "Apokatastasis in Coptic Texts from Nag Hammadi and Clement's and Origen's Apokatastasis: Toward an Assessment of the Origin of the Doctrine of Universal Restoration." *Journal of Coptic Studies* 14 (2014) 33–45.

Robinson, James M., ed. *The Nag Hammadi Library: The Definitive Translation of the Gnostic Scriptures Complete in One Volume*. 3rd ed. San Francisco: HarperSanFrancisco, 1990.

Rosenblum, Bruce, and Fred Kuttner. *Quantum Enigma: Physics Encounters Consciousness*. Oxford: Oxford University Press, 2011.

Schnackenburg, Rudolf. *The Gospel according to St. John*. Vol. 1. Translated by Kevin Smyth. Herder's Theological Commentary on the New Testament. 1968. Reprint, Montreal: Palm, 1982.

Scott, James C. *Domination and the Arts of Resistance: Hidden Transcripts*. New Haven: Yale University Press, 1990.

Suggs, M. Jack. *Wisdom, Christology, and Law in Matthew's Gospel*. Cambridge: Harvard University Press, 1970. Reprint, 2014.

Sullivan, J. W. N. "Interviews with the Great Scientists VI: Max Planck." *The Observer*, 25 Jan, 1931.

Taussig, Hal. *A New New Testament: A Bible for the Twenty-First Century*. Boston: Houghton Mifflin Harcourt, 2013.

Waldstein, Michael, and Frederik Wisse, eds. "The Apocryphon of John: Synopsis of Nag Hammadi Codices II, 1; III, 1; and IV, 1 with BG 8502,2." In *The Coptic Gnostic Library: A Complete Edition of the Nag Hammadi Codices*, vol. 2, edited by James M. Robinson, 12–177. Nag Hammadi and Manichaean Studies 33. Leiden: Brill, 1995.

Wheeler, John Archibald. "Frontiers of Time" (lecture, International School of Physics "Enrico Fermi," LXXII Course, Varenna, IT, Austin, TX, 1–5 August 1977). 10. https://jawarchive.files.wordpress.com/2012/02/frontiers-of-time-19781.pdf/.

Williams, Michael Allen. *The Immovable Race: A Gnostic Designation and the Theme of Stability in Late Antiquity.* Nag Hammadi Studies 29. Leiden: Brill, 1985.

———. *Rethinking "Gnosticism": An Argument for Dismantling a Dubious Category.* Princeton: Princeton University Press, 1996.

Wink, Walter. *The Powers That Be: Theology for a New Millennium.* New York: Doubleday, 1998.

General Index

Ancient Sources Index

CPSIA information can be obtained
at www.ICGtesting.com
Printed in the USA
BVHW061237090522
636528BV00004B/13

9 781666 730128